GENERAL EDITOR: JAMES GIBSON

Published

JANE AUSTEN	*Emma* Norman Page
	Sense and Sensibility Judy Simons
	Pride and Prejudice Raymond Wilson
	Mansfield Park Richard Wirdnam
SAMUEL BECKETT	*Waiting for Godot* Jennifer Birkett
WILLIAM BLAKE	*Songs of Innocence* and *Songs of Experience* Alan Tomlinson
ROBERT BOLT	*A Man for all Seasons* Leonard Smith
EMILY BRONTË	*Wuthering Heights* Hilda D. Spear
GEOFFREY CHAUCER	*The Miller's Tale* Michael Alexander
	The Pardoner's Tale Geoffrey Lester
	The Prologue to the Canterbury Tales Nigel Thomas and Richard Swan
CHARLES DICKENS	*Bleak House* Dennis Butts
	Great Expectations Dennis Butts
	Hard Times Norman Page
GEORGE ELIOT	*Middlemarch* Graham Handley
	Silas Marner Graham Handley
	The Mill on the Floss Helen Wheeler
HENRY FIELDING	*Joseph Andrews* Trevor Johnson
E. M. FORSTER	*Howards End* Ian Milligan
	A Passage to India Hilda D. Spear
WILLIAM GOLDING	*The Spire* Rosemary Sumner
	Lord of the Flies Raymond Wilson
OLIVER GOLDSMITH	*She Stoops to Conquer* Paul Ranger
THOMAS HARDY	*The Mayor of Casterbridge* Ray Evans
	Tess of the d'Urbervilles James Gibson
	Far from the Madding Crowd Colin Temblett-Wood
JOHN KEATS	*Selected Poems* John Garrett
PHILIP LARKIN	*The Whitsun Weddings* and *The Less Deceived* Andrew Swarbrick
D. H. LAWRENCE	*Sons and Lovers* R. P. Draper
HARPER LEE	*To Kill a Mockingbird* Jean Armstrong
CHRISTOPHER MARLOWE	*Doctor Faustus* David A. Male
THE METAPHYSICAL POETS	Joan van Emden

MACMILLAN MASTER GUIDES

THOMAS MIDDLETON and WILLIAM ROWLEY	*The Changeling* Tony Bromham
ARTHUR MILLER	*The Crucible* Leonard Smith
GEORGE ORWELL	*Animal Farm* Jean Armstrong
WILLIAM SHAKESPEARE	*Richard II* Charles Barber *Hamlet* Jean Brooks *King Lear* Francis Casey *Henry V* Peter Davison *The Winter's Tale* Diana Devlin *Julius Caesar* David Elloway *Macbeth* David Elloway *Measure for Measure* Mark Lilly *Henry IV Part I* Helen Morris *Romeo and Juliet* Helen Morris *The Tempest* Kenneth Pickering *A Midsummer Night's Dream* Kenneth Pickering
GEORGE BERNARD SHAW	*St Joan* Leonée Ormond
RICHARD SHERIDAN	*The School for Scandal* Paul Ranger *The Rivals* Jeremy Rowe
ALFRED TENNYSON	*In Memoriam* Richard Gill
JOHN WEBSTER	*The White Devil* and *The Duchess of Malfi* David A. Male

Forthcoming

CHARLOTTE BRONTË	*Jane Eyre* Robert Miles
JOHN BUNYAN	*The Pilgrim's Progress* Beatrice Batson
JOSEPH CONRAD	*The Secret Agent* Andrew Mayne
T. S. ELIOT	*Murder in the Cathedral* Paul Lapworth *Selected Poems* Andrew Swarbrick
GERARD MANLEY HOPKINS	*Selected Poems* R. Watt
BEN JONSON	*Volpone* Michael Stout
RUDYARD KIPLING	*Kim* Leonée Ormond
ARTHUR MILLER	*Death of a Salesman* Peter Spalding
JOHN MILTON	*Comus* Tom Healy
WILLIAM SHAKESPEARE	*Othello* Tony Bromham *As You Like It* Kiernan Ryan *Coriolanus* Gordon Williams *Antony and Cleopatra* Martin Wine
ANTHONY TROLLOPE	*Barchester Towers* Ken Newton
VIRGINIA WOOLF	*To the Lighthouse* John Mepham *Mrs Dalloway* Julian Pattison
W. B. YEATS	*Selected Poems* Stan Smith

MACMILLAN MASTER GUIDES
IN MEMORIAM
BY ALFRED TENNYSON

RICHARD GILL

MACMILLAN
EDUCATION

First edition 1987

Published by
MACMILLAN EDUCATION LTD
Houndmills, Basingstoke, Hampshire RG21 2XS
and London
Companies and representatives
throughout the world

Typeset by
TECSET, Sutton, Surrey

Printed in Hong Kong

British Library Cataloguing in Publication Data
Gill, Richard
In Memoriam by Alfred Tennyson.—
(Macmillan master guides)
1. Tennyson, Alfred Tennyson, *Baron*.
In Memoriam
I. Title
821'.8   PR5562
ISBN 0–333–42223–6 Pbk
ISBN 0–333–42224–4 Pbk export

To Mary

CONTENTS

GENERAL EDITOR'S PREFACE

The aim of the Macmillan Master Guides is to help you to appreciate the book you are studying by providing information about it and by suggesting ways of reading and thinking about it which will lead to a understanding. The section on the writer's life and background has has been designed to illustrate those aspects of the writer's life which have influenced the work, and to place it in its personal and literary context. The summaries and critical commentary are of special importance in that each brief summary of the action is followed by an examination of the significant critical points. The space which might have been given to repetitive explanatory notes has been devoted to a detailed analysis of the kind of passage which might confront you in an examination. Literary criticism is concerned with both the broader aspects of the work being studied and with its detail. The ideas which meet us in reading a great work of literature, and their relevance to us today, are an essential part of our study, and our Guides look at the thought of their subject in some detail. But just as essential is the craft with which the writer has constructed his work of art, and this may be considered under several technical headings – characterisation, language, style and stagecraft, for example.

The authors of these Guides are all teachers and writers of wide experience, and they have chosen to write about books they admire and know well in the belief that they can communicate their admiration to you. But you yourself must read and know intimately the book you are studying. No one can do that for you. You should see this book as a lamp-post. Use it to shed light, not to lean against. If you know your text and know what it is saying about life, and how it says it, then you will enjoy it, and there is no better way of passing an examination in literature.

JAMES GIBSON

ACKNOWLEDGEMENTS

I should like to thank James Gibson for his advice about the structure of the book, Adam Pokorny for his suggestions about Tennyson's poetic language, and Gillian Walters for her typing.

Cover illustration: *Remembrance of Johann Friedrich* by David Casper Friedrich. Photograph © Schloss Charlottenburg, West Berlin and by Courtesy of the Bridgeman Art Library.

A NOTE ON THE TEXT

The text used is that prepared by Susan Shatto and Marion Shaw and published by the Clarendon Press. The only conscious departure made is calling the opening verses the Prologue rather than Introductory stanzas.

1 TENNYSON AND HALLAM: LIFE AND BACKGROUND

In Memoriam, unlike most literary works, stands in a close, though not simple, relation to a historical event – the death in Vienna, on 15 September 1833, of Tennyson's friend, Arthur Henry Hallam. Tennyson received this news in a letter, dated 1 October, from Hallam's uncle, part of which read: 'He died at Vienna on his return from Buda, by Apoplexy – and I believe his Remains come by sea from Trieste.' The Tennysons were taking an early dinner when the letter arrived; Tennyson read it, left the room, went to see his sister Emily, to whom Hallam was engaged, told her the news and caught her as she fainted. On 6 October he wrote poem 9 of *In Memoriam*.

Hallam's death was, quite simply, the most significant event in Tennyson's life: a little pencil drawing of Hallam always hung over the fire-place wherever Tennyson lived; in 1852 he named his first son, Hallam, and on his death-bed in 1892 he is said to have called out 'Hallam, Hallam', but whether he was speaking to his devoted son or his long dead friend is a teasing ambiguity worthy of a poet.

In order to understand something of what Hallam meant to Tennyson, it is helpful to know a little of the poet's early life. His father, George, a clever, scholarly man, had been effectively disinherited by his rich father, so was forced to become a clergyman, whilst his younger brother was encouraged in a public career and eventually succeeded to, and re-built, Bayon's Manor – a rambling, romantic, many-turreted country mansion in Lincolnshire. By contrast, George brought up his large family (there were 12 children of whom the poet, Alfred, born in 1809, was the fourth) in Somersby Rectory, Lincolnshire. Life in that relatively small house was difficult, not only because the family knew it had been overlooked, but also because George Tennyson was an epileptic, a depressive, a taker of drugs, an alcoholic, and a man given to violence. School provided no relief;

Louth, which Alfred attended from the age of seven, was run by a sadist, who beat boys for the least misdemeanour.

Given such circumstances, it is surprising that there was any hilarity in the family, but, by common consent, they were a merry, eccentric family – George Tennyson took snuff in the pulpit, pondered for half an hour the question of which peg would be the most suitable one to hang his hat on, and the sons read and talked to themselves as they rambled the Lincolnshire lanes, an exercise they enjoyed both during the day and in the middle of the night.

Against such merriment and freedom there must be set the fact that Alfred's adolescence coincided with the sharpest decline in his father's health. It must, therefore, have been a relief for him to go up to Trinity College, Cambridge, in 1829. There he met Arthur Henry Hallam. Arthur's family background was a very different one. His father, Henry, was a much respected man; he was rich, influential in politics and a well-known historian. (The difference in their backgrounds may be of literary significance; it is notable that when Tennyson requires an image to express the gulf between the living and the dead he often turns to social class.) In spite of difference of class, wealth and education (Arthur attended Eton), the two were drawn together; both were poets (Tennyson and his brother, Charles, had already published, in 1827, *Poems by Two Brothers*), both were probably lonely, both had moments of fearing for their mental stability, and both had difficult fathers – Henry Hallam was quarrelsome and particularly demanding in educational matters. It might be said that their early lives had prepared them for friendship. The quality of that friendship was so rich that it is no exaggeration to say that after Hallam's death, Tennyson remained a wounded man for the rest of his life.

Hallam was believed by his friends to be exceptional. A. C. Bradley, summarising others' impressions, wrote of 'a very unusual completeness of character, of an equally rare absence of defects, and of a promise which seemed to his friends almost boundless'. Although he had been at school with Gladstone – arguably the most important politican of the Victorian period – contemporaries agreed that it was Arthur Hallam whom they believed would achieve most in the world. And Gladstone himself, towards the end of his life, said of Hallam that, among his contemporaries at Eton, 'he stood supreme', adding that 'the long life through which I have since wound my way and which has brought me into contact with so many men of rich endowments, leaves him where he then stood'.

Hallam introduced Tennyson to the Apostles – a group of undergraduates who met to discuss philosophical issues. Tennyson did not attend many meetings and on the one occasion when he promised to read an essay on Ghosts he failed to produce it. On another occasion the topic was whether the existence of God 'is deducible from the phenomena of the universe'. Both Hallam and Tennyson voted no. Such scepticism is in accord with the rhetorical yet agonised questioning in poems 54–56.

The two travelled abroad twice: to Spain in 1830, and the Rhine in 1833. They were undoubtedly happy journeys. Of the Spanish one Bernard Robert Martin, Tennyson's latest biographer, writes: 'It was the trip that meant most to Tennyson in all his life, one that he tried again and again to repeat as he remembered the pleasure of travelling with Hallam.' The experience of young men enjoying the companionship of walking may lie behind poems 22–26, in which the poet looks back upon a golden world of friendship, and two other poems, 71 and 98, refer to journeying through France and the Rhine Valley.

Their friendship was further deepened when Hallam met, fell in love with, and eventually proposed to, Tennyson's sister, Emily. (Poems 84 and the Epilogue touch on these matters.) Henry Hallam was hostile to the match and demanded a period of separation, but by 1832 (Hallam must have proposed late in 1830) their engagement was recognised. This enabled Hallam to spend his one and only Christmas at Somersby. There is no evidence as to what it was like, though the hollow, aching Christmas poems – 28–30, 78, 104–105 – suggest that, in sharp contrast to them, it was buoyant and full of joy.

Tennyson's friendship with Hallam must have been a source of great strength for him; nevertheless, family troubles continued. Even before he went to Cambridge it had been suggested that his father should be committed to a lunatic asylum, and although that course was not adopted, George Tennyson did go into voluntary exile on the continent, returning home in July 1830. He died at Somersby in March 1831. But 1833 was the blackest year for the family in general, and Alfred in particular. In that year his brother Edward was committed, as it turned out for the rest of his life, to a lunatic asylum in York, and it became known that Charles, Alfred's favourite brother (poem 79 is addressed to him), was hopelessly addicted to opium. And then there were the stinging reviews. His *Poems Chiefly Lyrical* (1830) was roughed up in *Blackwood's Magazine*, and in April J. W. Croker savaged *Poems* (1833). In October came the news of Hallam's death.

It has already been stated that one of Tennyson's responses to Hallam's death was the writing of poetry. In the early days he wrote three, 9, 30, 31, and by 1834 he had composed two distinct, though incomplete, groups – one about the return of the boat and the other about the first Christmas and Lazarus. This means that Tennyson's later remark – 'I did not write them with any view of weaving them into a whole, or for publication, until I found so many' – can't be wholly right, because the 'weaving' had clearly begun within a few months of Hallam's death. The number of individual poems grew steadily. By 1840 there were over 60 and by the late 1840s over 100. A private trial edition consisting of 119 poems appeared in March 1850, and what is usually called the First Edition appeared in June of the same year. It comprised a 129 poems. Poem 59 was added in 1851, and with the addition of number 39 in 1870 it was complete.

There is something almost symbolic about the poem's publication: *In Memoriam* was published on 1 June 1850 – a central date in the year and the century for what, with hindsight, is the central poetic work of the Victorian age. It was widely and favourably reviewed, sold very well (there were three editions within four months), touched the popular imagination and established Tennyson as unquestionably the foremost poet of the age. In November 1850 he was offered and accepted the post of Poet Laureate.

The poem is not simply an account of a friendship. One of its features is that events *after* the death of Hallam stand behind some of its individual sections. The burial of Hallam (which Tennyson did not attend) at Clevedon in Somerset is the occasion of poem 18. Poem 87 may be based upon a visit to Cambridge in March 1838. The honeymoon of Tennyson's brother Charles, and his wife Louisa, is possibly the origin of 98. In October 1837 the Tennysons left Somersby for High Beech, Epping Forest; poems 100–103 appear to be prompted by this. The Epilogue is a poem occasioned by the marriage of his sister Cecilia to Tennyson's friend, Edmund Lushington in October 1842.

Two warnings must be made about identifying events behind the poems. The first is that, if an event did occasion a poem, it does not follow that the actual composition closely followed the event. Poem 102, for instance, may have been written about two years after the move from Somersby. The second point follows from this. Even if a poem was occasioned by an identifiable event, readers should not assume that *In Memoriam* is a record. Tennyson was concerned with expressing the feelings and significances he found in events, not with an accurate description of them.

This has an important bearing on the matter of the poem's huge popularity. *In Memoriam* is one of those works of art in which an author, by thinking over what is of the utmost *personal* concern to him or her, touches upon what is of *general* concern to very many people. In short, from what is intensely private there springs that which is publicly central. *In Memoriam* expressed feelings, tried to formulate significances and asked questions that many readers felt, spoke and asked or, from their own state of puzzled inarticulacy, struggled towards.

There were features in contemporary culture that enabled readers to sympathise with the stance of the poet in the poem. The first was a growing preoccupation, stimulated by religious doubts, with death. The crisis of faith had many causes: the alienation of the urban masses from the Church, the growth of an historical approach to the Bible, the emergence of philosophies that were positivistic in tone in that they sought to exclude any metaphysical or transcendental categories, and the findings of science, particularly in biology and geology, which apparently questioned the Biblical record and, thereby, undermined the truths of the Christian faith. One of the manifestations of doubt was an anxiety about death: did the soul survive the death of the body? Was it possible to meet our loved ones after death? Do the dead watch over us? These questions, which were wrenched from people's hearts with a peculiarly intense anguish, appear in, or stand behind, *In Memoriam*. The poem, therefore, takes its place alongside other characteristic expresions of this pervasive anxiety: touching death-bed scenes in novels, the popularity of spiritualism, lengthy and expensive rituals of family mourning, and huge sculptured mausoleums that stand thickly together in enormous municipal cemeteries.

Those who doubted sought comfort. Victorian society demanded, and consequently created, authoritative guides. This is the second feature which inclined readers to be sympathetic to *In Memoriam*. A word that is often used of these guide figures is 'sage', another is 'hero'. Beset by doubts, people looked to a sage to articulate the problems, show that he or she was also troubled by them, and offer some comfort by proposing solutions. A particularly interesting aspect of this need was that in the middle years of the century literary figures – poets, novelists, essayists – began to assume in people's minds the role and status once held exclusively by the clergy. The historian, W. E. H. Lecky, wrote in 1860: 'It is our lay writers who are moulding the characters and forming the opinions of the age; they have superseded the clergy in the direction of the thought of England.' It is not surprising that a poem in which someone openly and heroically wrestles with death should have appealed to a reading public nagged by religious doubt and in need of consolation.

The above sentence raises a question which is critical as well as historical: who is the 'someone' who wrestles with death? The danger of an historical approach is that it leads to a simple identification of the 'I' of the poem with Alfred Tennyson. Tennyson himself recognised this as problematic. '"I" is not always the author speaking of himself, but the voice of the human race speaking through him.' Tennyson's point is that sometimes the poem works autobiographically and sometimes representatively. Another of his remarks is even firmer; In Memoriam is 'a poem, not an actual biography.' As was said at the start of this chapter, the poem stands in a close, though not simple, relation to certain events. In the commentary that follows the current convention will be adopted of referring to the voice in the poem as 'the poet' and using the name 'Tennyson' when discussing matters of design and style. There are dangers of inflexbility in this, though it should be pointed out that it is usually obvious when Tennyson and the poetic 'I' merge, so readers can make the necessary critical adjustments.

Because of the very special and quite complex relationship between Tennyson's experiences and In Memoriam, his life after 1850 is not of direct relevance to a study of the poem. In the literary field it saw him constantly experimenting; Maud, a long poem of astonishing power, was published in 1855, and Idylls of the King, an English epic consisting of long poems based upon the legends of King Arthur's court, was first published in 1859, republished in 1862 with a dedication to the late Prince Albert, Queen Victoria's husband, published again with new poems and an Epilogue To the Queen in 1872 and completed in 1874. 1875 saw the publication of Queen Mary, his first play. An aspect of In Memoriam that is present in many of his later works is the tension between the private and the public. In Maud, for instance, the intensely vivid exploration of a mind on the verge of insanity has as its background the Crimean War.

Tennyson's life after 1850 was, at least on the surface, strikingly successful. He received many public honours, the most notable of which was a baronetcy which, after three refusals, he finally accepted in 1883. He travelled, moved in high circles, was a member of the Metaphysical Society (a group of prominent thinkers) and, perhaps a symbolic gesture aimed at restoring the Tennyson family's reputation, had a big house, Aldworth, built for himself in Surrey. After his death in 1892 he was buried in Westminster Abbey. But in spite of such achievements, the image he presented to the world was of a man not at ease with himself. The writer Thomas Carlyle said that he carried about with him 'a bit of chaos'. It is easy to understand the truth of that statement from the photographs, portraits and statues of him; they show a gaunt, brooding and even haunted man, who, to adopt the words of poem 57 of In Memoriam, had left half his life behind him when his friend had died.

2 COMMENTARY ON

IN MEMORIAM

2.1 THE DESIGN OF THE POEM

It is inevitable that readers faced with a long poem are going to ask questions about its design. Some may wonder whether there is a scheme which controls all its individual sections, some may look for a major turning point, whilst others may look for common features which give an emotional, intellectual or imaginative unity. Tennyson, in conversation with a friend, once proposed a nine part division: 1–8, 9–20, 21–37, 38–49, 50–58, 59–71, 72–98, 99–103, 104–131. However, he never elaborated upon this, and, moreover, the division ignores the second Christmas poem (78). To many people this is a fatal objection; *In Memoriam*, as far as its time-scale is concerned, is plotted around three Christmases – 28–30, 78, 104–5 – and three springs – 38–39, 86 and 88, 115–116.

A much more popular account of the poem's design was given by A. C. Bradley in his *A Commentary on Tennyson's In Memoriam*. His division accepts the centrality of the Christmas poems and picks out shorter, connected sequences ('distinct groups') within longer sections. This is a summary of it:

Part I:	To The First Christmas		
	Poems 1–27		
		9–17 or 20	The ship poems
		22–25	A retrospect of friendship
Part II:	To The Second Christmas		
	Poems 28–77	28–30	Christmastide.
		31–36	Faith in immortality.
		40–47	Possibility of future reunion.

Two things must be stressed about Bradley's division. The first is that in his commentary it emerges as a more subtle scheme than the above summary suggests. The second is that he recognises that some of the poems are much more loosely related to each other than others, which have a strong narrative or discursive thread.

The above point is very important. It must be said very firmly that readers who are expecting to find a clear scheme in the poem are going to be disappointed. It must also be said that those who look for a clear, step by step development from grief to hope are not going to find one. What is both moving and convincing about *In Memoriam* is its fragmentary quality. Tennyson called the poem the 'Way of the Soul'. It is not forcing the analogy of the path or road to say that the way pursued in this poem is uneven; it twists and turns, reaches emotional heights and then sinks to the depths and even turns back on itself. This moves the reader because the poet is always vulnerable, and is convincing because, in anyone's emotional life, states of elation or depression rarely last for long, and even when, over a period of months or years, the mind gradually reaches contentment or sinks into hopelessness, the actual passage to the state is full of lapses – surprising moments of happiness or unaccountable phases of gloom. This aspect of *In Memoriam*, the way it follows an ever changing emotional contour, is in part due to the fact that there is no abrupt change in the poem. Number 95 is a crucial poem but, significantly, that vision is followed by a poem about doubt. Such a sequence is intellectually and emotionally credible. The human mind can swing from one state to another, and moments of assurance are often followed by acute questioning. It is interesting to note in this connection that some contemporary readers and reviewers spoke about the 'intuitive' character of the poem.

What a reader should expect, then, is a collection of poems of different types – stories, arguments, imaginary conversations, scenes from nature – some of which have strong connections with each other and some of which do not. They are connected in various ways – by contrast, the association of a single word, by argument, by narrative, by mood – and they form, not a scheme, but a long, uneven and bitty kind of personal diary full of scraps, jottings and speculations.

The division of the poem that the rest of the commentary follows is a new one, though it owes much to Bradley. It is not proposed as a 'solution' to the problem of the poem's design, but offered as another way of understanding the winding emotional and intellectual course of *In Memoriam*.

2.2 IN MEMORIAM

Prologue

Since, with the exception of 39, the Prologue (sometimes called Introductory stanzas) was the last poem to be written, it can be read as a commentary upon the whole work rather than as an integral part of it. Thus it is concerned with life, death, human limitation, faith knowledge, forgiveness and poetry. It is sometimes felt to be too bland and assured, but even the apparently firm opening stanza can be read as an expression of doubt and uncertainty:

> Strong Son of God, immortal Love,
>> Whom we, that have not seen thy face,
>> By faith, and faith alone, embrace,
> Believing where we cannot prove;

The choice of words to characterise Christ – 'Strong', 'immortal Love' – looks more like expressions of what the poet needs to believe than language which is appropriate to prayer. In an age of doubt there is a need for a strong figure upon whom people can rely, and, as shall be seen, since the poet desperately wants to believe that his love will never die, it comes naturally to him to call Christ 'immortal Love'. The need to be assured is evident in the second line, where the poet places himself and his readers in the position of doubting Thomas, the disciple who would not believe in the resurrection unless he saw the risen Christ. The need and the doubt may account for the strain felt in the over-emphatic insistence of 'By faith, and faith alone, embrace'. 'Faith alone' is a common phrase in religious circles, but here it borders on despair. In effect, the poet is saying: this is all we have. 'Embrace', too, is equivocal. In that it reminds the reader of the kiss with which Judas betrayed Christ it has sinister undertones, but it is also disturbingly inappropriate in another way: the very physical and even amorous associations the word has point the reader away from Christ to the earthly friendship between the poet and his late friend. It is as if the poet's mind is wandering while he prays. The last line is an example of the subtlest undermining of overt confidence. 'Believing' is, in grammatical terms, a participle, whereas 'we cannot prove' is a verb in a negated form. Because participles are related to verbs but don't perform all their functions (a sentence with just a participle and no verb is not really a sentence) they are considered weaker forms. In the last line the positive – 'believing' – is therefore less strong than the negative – 'we cannot prove'. The first stanza, then, is much less assured than a quick reading might suggest. Consequently, it is a quite appropriate introduction to the whole poem.

The Prologue introduces another very important aspect of the poem. The oddness of the first line's language has been noted, and a reason for it has been advanced. If that reason is explored, it becomes evident that the Prologue (and much of the rest of the poem) is an expression, not of orthodox Christianity, but of the religion that comes naturally to an ordinary person who knows little or no theology and may not even care to know. Christ (who is not named as such) only 'seemest human and divine', and man merely 'thinks he was not made to die'. This, for many readers, makes the poem both moving and noble. The poet is a searcher, an inquirer who does not assume the truth of, or easily resort to, traditional Christian formulations. In the darkness of his doubt he lamely admits that 'we have but faith: we cannot know', so all he can do is 'trust it comes from thee'. He also asks for something that, in its day, must have seemed more impressive to some readers than faith – knowledge. The very way he asks for it is fraught with strain in that the plea for both knowledge and reverence stretches over from one stanza to another. The desired harmony is thus made to seem a very remote possibility:

> May make one music as before,
> But vaster.

The poem concludes with three sentences all of which commence with 'Forgive'. What needs forgiveness is his 'sin', his 'grief' and his 'wild and wandering cries'. The last is a reference to his poetry. That is a subject to which the whole poem will frequently return.

1–8

These poems, dealing with the initial impact of bereavement, resemble entries in a diary: the poet walks to the churchyard and sees a Yew among the graves (2), reflects on the aimlessness of nature (3), is subject to 'nameless trouble' crossing his mind as he sleeps (4), writes poetry (5), receives letters (6), visits the house of his dead friend (7) and, thinking of others who have suffered, resolves to pay a poetic tribute (8).

Their bleak atmosphere is carefully created. The bereaved poet occupies an apparently empty world: nature is 'a hollow echo' and 'a hollow form' (3); 'He is not here' is sadly proclaimed (7), and in 8 'chambers [are] emptied of delight'. It is also a dark world: 'darkness keep(s) her raven gloss' (1); the Yew tree exists 'in the dusk' (2); his will is 'bondsman to the dark' (4), and to the poet 'all is dark where thou art not.' (8). Sounds are subdued ('whispers' is used twice in 3), except when the silence is broken by 'a cry' (3) or the meaningless 'noise of life' (7).

The mood might be called subterranean; it is as if the mind of the poet is dead and buried. He is fascinated by, and even longs for, the life of the Yew, which grows above 'the under-lying dead' and whose fibres 'net the dreamless head' and 'are wrapt about the bones'. In sleep 'clouds of nameless trouble cross/All night below the darken'd eyes' (4), and poetry is a relief, like a narcotic, because it 'half conceal[s] the Soul within' (5), and the poet can wrap himself in words 'like coarsest clothes'.

The first poem, however, does not open in tones of dark introspection:

> I held it truth, with him who sings
> To one clear harp in divers tones,
> That men may rise on stepping-stones
> Of their dead selves to higher things.

Although the image of the last two lines is confused (people cross things on stepping-stones rather than rising on them), it provides a hopeful direction for the poem. The poet believes, though how confidently can be judged by the change from the firm 'held' to the less certain 'may', that either what is dead in people, or their former selves killed by harsh experience, can be a stage in a progress to 'higher things'. Thus the possibility of moving from despair to hope is stated at the very start. In fact, poem 1 anticipates the jubilant 130 in which the poet says 'My love involves the love before' and 'I seem to love thee more and more.'

But the possibility of far-off happiness gives way to what might be thought unhealthy self-indulgence. Because it is hard to 'reach a hand thro' time' (the first of many occasions in the poem when friendship is presented in terms of a hand reaching for, or touching, another) the poet, instead, asks 'Love [to] clasp Grief lest both be drown'd'. The poet actually wants to maintain his intense grief, because otherwise his love would be lost as his grief sinks. This willed rejection of comfort (the poetry of the natural man rather than the orthodox Christian) is embodied in a striking line – 'Let darkness keep her raven gloss'. 'Raven gloss' suggests an attractively polished surface of something which is rich and costly. And that is how the poet wants his grief; it must be shiny and new, not, to adopt the last word of the poem, 'overworn'.

The desire to persist in grief finds an even more appropriate image in the Yew, which is both in contact with the dead and apparently unchanging through the seasons. The poet is impressed by its 'thousand years of gloom' and 'stubborn hardihood' and he seems to grow 'incorporate' into the tree. It is a state he longs for; to 'fail out' of his 'blood' is not just to die but to escape from all that the word 'blood' means – the ebb and flow of emotion. If he becomes a part of the tree he will always remain in his present state of grief.

Yet even in this numbed state there is a growth in feeling. This is explored in poem 6 where he receives letters, one of which says that 'Loss is common to the race'. He rejects this idea by using repetition as an instrument of devaluation – 'And common is the common-place, – but still moves on to consider the common fate of all who are bereaved – the father, the mother and the young girl. This is the first moment in the poem when the poet sees his own grief in terms of others, and, significantly, the grief that has been 'shaken into frost' (4) breaks out in sympathy. Perhaps the most moving moment in 6 for both poet and reader is the poignant section on the young girl, who 'takes a riband *or* a rose' unaware that such a trivial choice coincides with much grimmer alternatives for her beloved, who 'was drown'd in passing thro'the ford/*Or* kill'd in falling from his horse.'

Nevertheless, in spite of the movement of sympathy in 6, poems 1–8 will be remembered for their brooding, unappeased grief. A grief that is so hauntingly expressed in the barren townscape of poem 7, where 'life' is reduced to a 'noise' heard 'far away', and the dawn, a conventional symbol of hope and new life, is pictured in this bleak line – 'On the bald street breaks the blank day.'

9–21

This section deals with the return by sea of the body of the dead friend, and his burial in land overlooking the Severn Estuary. It resembles 1–8 in that both deal with a sequence of events and conclude with reflections on poetry. Yet there are important differences. In poem 7 the poet was actually present at his friend's house, whereas in 10, 12, 13 and 17 he travels in imagination to see the ship. The tones are quite different: 1–8 is deadened and subdued (subterranean), while 9–21, with the exception of violent eruptions in 15 and 16, is, to use words from the poems, 'placid' (9), 'gentle' (9), 'quiet' (10) and 'calm' (11). And closely related to tone is atmosphere: there is a movement away from the rawness of the 'bald street' to 'the high wold' (11) and 'the pleasant shore' (19).

The scenes in 9–21 are predominantly natural; that is to say, there are landscapes and seascapes. This creates one of the most interesting problems in the poem. In this section and elsewhere, Tennyson shows that he has a sharp eye and an acute ear. Consider the following lines:

Ruffle thy mirror'd mast . . . (9)

The chestnut pattering to the ground (11)

That twinkle into green and gold (11)

The rooks are blown about the skies (15)

And makes a silence in the hills (19)

The sights and sounds of nature are perceptively captured, and in all five lines the rhythms and sounds subtly enact their subjects without being blunderingly onomatopoeic. But a question must be asked: are such beauties entirely separate from the expressions of grief? In other words, is Tennyson doing two entirely unrelated things – sensitively evoking the beauties of nature and writing about the feelings of bereavement?

The problem of relating landscape to grief is starkly present in poem 11. The remarkably stable sentence structure (each verse has virtually identical grammar) creates the calm of which the poem speaks. Moreover, the first stanza does make a connection between the calm of the morning and the 'calmer grief' the poet feels. The calm atmosphere is sustained in the subsequent stanzas, and, more importantly, the reader is invited to see links between natural landscape and the poet's state of mind. For instance, the 'great plain' with its 'crowded farms and lessening towers' eventually 'mingle[s]' with the bounding main', thereby comfortingly suggesting a future in which the poet will merge with the encompassing sea of death and so meet his friend. What Tennyson does there is draw on the Romantic tradition of nature verse in which a landscape is partly the expression of the feelings of the one who views it. To put it briefly: natural landscape is mental landscape. But such a way of viewing the natural world is radically undermined by the shock of the closing stanza:

> Calm on the seas, and silver sleep,
> And waves that sway themselves in rest,
> And dead calm in that noble breast
> Which heaves but with the heaving deep.

That is a black parody of Romantic verse. It's as if the poet is saying: if you want a relationship between landscape and feeling, I'll show you how the sea mimes a corpse – the body heaves up and down not through any life in it but just because it's on 'the heaving deep.' Perhaps the Romantic tradition of establishing a relationship between landscape and feeling breaks down when the subject is that which removes all feeling – death. This much is certain: whatever is possible later in the poem, number 11 shows the inability of the poet to see the outer world of nature matching the inner world of feeling in a comforting manner.

There is, however, more to this section than that problem. One feature is a new way in which the poet speaks of bereavement. Twice he says 'Till all my widow'd race be run' (9, 17) and in 13 he pictures himself as the widower moving his 'doubtful arms' only to discover 'her place' in bed is 'empty'. (The image of man and wife recurs throughout *In Memoriam*.) There is clearly a relationship between the 'widower' image and the use of words concerned with physical contact such as 'touch' and 'clasp'.

Another feature of these poems is related to the matter of physical contact. The popularity of the poem is surely in part due to the way it relates to a deeply-held, though obscure, feeling that the bodies of our dead are still precious to us. Hence the poet fears that if the boat sinks his friend will 'toss with tangle and with shells' (10). 'Tangle' captures the feeling that if that were to happen it would be as if his friend had been imprisoned in a confusion of writhing tendrils. Given that the poem does touch upon the fear that the body might be lost, there is a welcome, though subdued, sense of relief in the lines about burial:

> 'Tis well: 'tis something; we may stand
> Where he in English earth is laid (18)

The dead one is safe and we, the living, may still establish contact with him by standing at his grave. The lines are both sad and yet comforting.

22–27

Unlike earlier poems, these ones explore the past rather than the present. In a conventional metaphor – the path of life – the poet, 'looking back to whence I came' (23), sees the 'fair companionship' (22) he enjoyed when 'all we met was fair and good' (23). They also mark the appearance of the friend. Until now he has been an absence – 'A hand that can be clasp'd no more' (7) and 'a vanish'd life' (10). When the imaginary critic in 21 complained about the excessive devotion of the poet, the reply was: 'Ye never knew the sacred dust'. Such a statement is true of the reader as well as the critic. Perhaps that is the reason the poet now includes him.

Two pieces of grammar help to express the appearance of the friend. The first is the use of the first person plural – the path is one on which 'we twain did go', and '*we* with singing cheer'd the way' (22). When, however, 'the path we walk'd began/To slant the fifth autumnal slope', the Shadow 'feared of man' – death – broke 'our fair companionship' and, also, broke the grammar down into lonely singulars – 'And bore *thee* where *I* could not see'. Plurals return in 23 but that is because it is a reminiscence of the past. It is a useful study examining singulars and plurals in the poem. Sometimes, for instance, plurals appear but often they are anonymous and even impersonal.

The second piece of grammar is what will be called reciprocal syntax – a word order that answers itself either by repetition of words, sentence structure, or thought, and thereby establishes the 'fair companionship' of the young men. In 22 the years are 'crown'd' with goodness as they 'cheer'd the way':

> From April on to April went,
> And glad at heart from May to May:

April answers April and May May, and the structure of the lines answer each other in the parallel phrasing of 'From April on to April' and 'from May to May'. (It must also be said that the satisfying harmony of that last line is due to the playful positioning of the crucial word 'heart' at the heart of the line.)In 23 the reciprocal syntax is even more striking, for the verbs express the interchange of mind and phrase:

> When each by turns was guide to each,
> And Fancy light from Fancy caught,
> And Thought leapt out to wed with Thought
> Ere Thought could wed itself with Speech;

Each 'by turns' (virtually a description of reciprocal syntax) was 'guide' to each, so 'Fancy' can catch a thought from 'Fancy', and the consequence of 'Thought' leaping out to 'Thought' is that Thought can 'wed itself' with Speech. In the final verb the two parallel lines of the central couplet are indeed 'wed' together. It is another playful piece of poetic self-consciousness.

It is appropriate that at this point the poetry is exhilaratingly youthful; its playfulness and self-consciousness has something in it of the exuberant showiness of youth. Poems 22 and 23 celebrate the joy of discovering a friend. Even the conventional metaphor of the path is brought to life through a contrast with prison – 'Now, sometimes in my sorrow shut' – and through an anticipated contrast with 'sloth' in 27. The freedom of the road (it is reminiscent of William Wordsworth's journeys through France in Book 6 of *The Prelude*) allows the poet to express himself ('The murmur of a happy Pan') and together they discover that 'many an old philosophy' (Hallam was more of a philosopher than a poet) can come alive for them and sing on 'Argive heights'.

But death is not far away. Poem 22 turns itself into a Bunyanesque allegory, when with 'the fifth autumnal slope' they enter Tennyson's version of the Valley of the Shadow of Death. Death 'spread his mantle dark and cold,/And wrapt thee formless in the fold'. The language is troubled. 'Formless' might suggest release (the advanced intellectual in 33 who has reached 'a purer air' cares not to fix his belief 'to form') but it also means the poet can no longer establish contact with his friend through touch. 'Fold' is also difficult. To the poet Death has stolen his friend, but if readers cannot fail to see in 'fold' a suggestion of the sheepfold protected by Christ, the Good Shepherd, then it is clear that the poet has not accepted the consolation of religion.

Death brings doubt. Significantly, however, it is short lived. After the poet has entertained some commonplace ideas that suggest that their friendship was not as idyllic as he imagined he strenuously affirms: 'I know that this was Life' (25). Life did prepare 'The daily burden for the back' but the poet loved the burden 'Because it needed help of love'. Affirmations continue. 26 repeats the request of poem 1 that his love should never die, and in 27 he adopts the role of a man who loudly protests that, for all his pain, he would not have had life otherwise. To modern ears the tone of voice might seem strident and the thought unoriginal (there are several Latin models for it), but to understand *In Memoriam* a reader must try to do justice both to its felt passion and to its attempt to think through problems in a public language that many can share. After a number of emblematic examples which are given added significance by the definite article – 'The captive', 'The linnet', 'the beast' – the poem mounts to this climax:

> I hold it true, whate'er befall;
> I feel it, when I sorrow most;
> 'Tis better to have loved and lost
> Than never to have loved at all.

The rhetorical pose ('I hold it true' could come from the pulpit), the sweeping gesture of 'whate'er befall', the conclusive intensity of 'I feel it' and the clarity of the final two lines are all expressive of a deeply-held assurance. And, moreover, the stanza, unlike the preceding poems, is in the present tense. This is a creed the poet has, not one he once held.

There is a discernible pattern in 22–27 of experience recalled, experience doubted, and experience reaffirmed; it is a pattern the whole poem aspires to affirm but, as many of the following poems will show, one which is not easily achieved.

28–39

These poems deal with the first Christmas following the friend's death, the story of Lazarus, the relationship of faith to reason and the first spring. Since the subjects, though varied, form a clear sequence, the poems will be examined in order.

The Christmas poems (28–30) are domestic and thus recall the imagery of 6, 8, and 20; there is mention, for instance, of 'the holly round the Christmas hearth' (30) and 'our old pastimes in the hall'. Because Christmas is a time of family gatherings, and remembering the past, the poignancy of the poet's loss is all the more keenly felt. The bells 'bring me sorrow touch'd with joy' (28) and not, as he might have said, joy touched with sorrow. Christmas in these poems is strangely unlike itself. In 28 'The moon is hid', so there is no symbolism of light, and although the bells momentarily revive the use of reciprocal syntax – 'The Christmas bells from hill to hill' – the following line undercuts any harmony because they 'Answer each other in the mist.' The third stanza attempts a lively responsiveness but this time the sombre rhyme of the central couplet 'decrease,/ peace' does exactly that. The other grammatical feature of 22–28 – plurals – returns but, instead of the mutual companionship of the young, it is used of a family still numb from grief. The poet even asks: 'How dare we keep our Christmas-eve' (29). They do, but instead of the 'merry song we sang with him' (30), there is the mechanical activity, created by the repeated 'and', of 'dance and song and game and jest' (29). Perhaps the most telling instance of the departed glow of meaning is the line about 'the cold baptismal font' (29) entwined with holly boughs. No longer is the font associated with purification and new life; it has become an object of antiquity which is 'cold' to both the touch and the mind. Christmas without the friend has been eroded to its symbolic meaning; it is merely a desacralised season of oppressive weather and falling spirits: 'A rainy cloud possess'd the earth/And sadly fell our Christmas-eve' (30).

Like the Christmas poems, the ones about Lazarus (31–32) are about a family. Their most important link, however, is the hope raised in 30 that the dead do not 'lose their mortal sympathy'. This hope, which may well be the most deeply held one in the entire poem (it is central to 40–49), is the impetus behind Mary's question as to whether her brother 'yearn'd/To hear her weeping by his grave?' The yearning is not just to know that life is not extinguished by death, but to be assured that the dead still hear and care for the living. The figure of Lazarus haunted the death-troubled Victorians (Robert Browning wrote 'An Epistle of Karshish' on the same subject): here was 'a man raised up by Christ!' and yet either he was not asked the crucial question – 'Where wert thou, brother, those four days?' – or he did give an answer but 'something seal'd/The lips of that Evangelist.' He was, in short, the one figure who might have revealed to humanity the secrets that lie beyond death, but he remained tantalisingly silent on the subject.

The example of Mary whose gladness subdues 'subtle thought' and 'curious fears' (32) prompts speculation about faith, reason and immortality. In 33 a thinker who is ripe in reason and holds to 'the law within' is warned not to denigrate his sister's simpler faith with its 'early Heaven' and 'happy views'. The vagueness of the person addressed may indicate that the poet (or Tennyson) has himself in mind. This is supported by poems 34 and 35 which are exercises, conducted by the poet, in reasoning about immortality. The poet, as so often in the poem, conducts a dialogue with himself, the outcome of which is not a philosophical conclusion but images, one of death and the other of unbridled lust, which are intended to shock the reader into recognising the impossibility of living without the hope of immortality.

Thinking in images prepares the reader for poems 36 and 37. 36 is the most positive statement so far about conventional religion. The Gospels are universal ('Which he may read that binds the sheaf') because in them 'truth [is] embodied in a tale'. It is very much a poet's justification for religion. 37 is a difficult poem in which Urania, the muse of heavenly poetry, and Melpomene, the muse of tragedy, criticise and encourage the poet (*In Memoriam* is a poem full of voices and dialogues) in his work. The issue is whether the poet should explore the profound matters investigated in the previous four poems, so it shows that self-doubt is not absent.

The image in 37 of the pastoral poet wandering by his 'native rill' revives the image of the path, which is used again in 38. In spite of the spring, usually a symbol of a renewed inner life, the poet 'loiter[s] on' with 'weary steps'. The sense of living a life bereft of joy and meaning recalls the flat tones of 26 – 'Still onward winds the dreary way/I with it'. The reader may imagine this aimless wandering taking the poet into the churchyard, where he, once again, contemplates the Yew. Because the poem convincingly plots the ever changing contours of grief, the tone of the earlier poem is re-established. There is, for instance, the darkly impressive and almost subliminal connection between the Yew and the sea. In 2 its fibres 'net the dreamless head', while in 39 the words are: 'dippest toward the dreamless head'. The association between grief and sea recalls poems 9–17 and suggests, to use Matthew Arnold's words from his poem 'Dover Beach', 'the turbid ebb and flow/Of human misery.' Nevertheless, true to the constant change of emotions that characterises *In Memoriam*, there is a moment of brightness given in an attempt to revive reciprocal syntax:

> To these too comes the golden hour
> When flower is feeling after flower

In the phrase 'feeling after' there is an impulse to respond to the renewal of the spring, but the promised new life, in a characteristically dark falling cadence, 'passes into gloom again' at the close of the poem.

40–49

Two wishes dominate the early parts of *In Memoriam*: the wish that the poet's love for his friend may never weaken, and the wish that the dead friend will be able to think of the living. The second of these wishes is the impetus behind all the poems of this section except 48 and 49, which are reflections on the preceding ones. Because they are reflections, it is helpful to begin with one of them.

48 opens with a probing subjunctive – 'If these brief lays . . .' – about the status of what has been said. It is not 'Sorrow's' aims to 'part and prove' but to take any doubt that 'may flit,/And make it vassal unto love'. Two images fuse themselves in those lines: 'vassal' is concerned with freedom, slavery and the social order, and 'flit', the light movement of something which flies, anticipates the image in the closing stanza:

> Short swallow-flights of song, that dip
> Their wings in tears, and skim away.

The poems in this section are 'swallow-flights'; that is, glancing, exploratory skimmings that approach their subject from a multiplicity of angles, doing no more than lightly touch upon the surface of the issue. Poems 40–47 are, therefore, a series of oblique searchings. The poet skims from image to image in the hope of finding an adequate way of imagining the life of the dead and their relations to the living. Hitherto, *In Memoriam* has depended upon conventional poetic ideas – life as a path, death as sleep – but it is important to recognise that it is an innovative and speculative, as well as a traditional, poem. It is, in fact, a poem (both here and elsewhere) in search of a poetic language adequate to its subject matter. In a number of poems the poet 'sports with words' and hopes that his art will 'glance,/Like light' (49).

Poem 40 starts with a proposal to understand the gulf between the living and the dead as being like that between a girl before and after marriage. The image is explored in detail for five stanzas, until the poet breaks it off with this admission – 'Ay me, the difference I discern!' The image is inadequate, so he turns to a familiar one to end the poem – the path:

> My paths are in the fields I know,
> And thine in undiscover'd lands.

But this image has its shortcomings. Because the dead walk in 'undiscover'd lands' the imagination must be unsure about the course it plots.

41 and 42 also show efforts (not always sucessful) to find an adequate language. In 41 the path gives way to an image of ascent, which, in turn, becomes that of the altar-fire. The poet, however, admits that he has 'lost the links that bound/Thy changes'. Those words could apply to the poetry itself, because the image of a chain – 'links' – is much too materialistic to convey the relationship between the living and the dead. The language of 42 is vague. The image of the race is clear, but 'Place' is quite misty. It looks as if Tennyson has in mind a large country house where 'A lord of large experience, [may] train/To riper growth the mind and will' but he could also be imagining a heavenly version of a Cambridge college. This frustrating lack of specificity shows that the right poetic language has not been discovered.

In 43 and 44 Tennyson needs images that will express the poet's hope that even in that 'high place' (44) his friend will remember him. He explores a number of images. 43 starts with 'Sleep and Death' and moves gradually into a quasi-allegorical image of 'that still garden of the souls' where in 'the spiritual prime' (so different from the spring of 38) the 'dawning soul' will wake to find 'silent traces of the past'. In 44 the crucial point is the hope that 'some dim touch of earthly things' may 'surprise' the friend when he is 'ranging' with his 'peers'. None of these images is new. What Tennyson is doing is transforming the image of the touch of friendship and the path. The fact that he can't forget them is a sign of how much they mean to him.

45 introduces yet another image – the growing child who gradually discovers his own sense of identity. The image is developed for three stanzas and then (a sign that Tennyson is less than confident about it?) the mood changes as a conclusion is wrenched from it. The argument appears to be that since 'blood and breath' form the self with its clear memory, there would be no point in this process if, after

death, the whole thing had to be repeated. Hence, logic rudely interrupts the image in order to prove that memory must survive death.

46 revives and transforms the image of the path. The poet has assured himself that the dead do remember, so, with great speculative daring, he charts what 'The eternal landscape of the past' must look like to the dead. Their friendship is seen as 'A bounded field', but because Venus, the star of love, looks over it the field becomes 'A rosy warmth from marge to marge.' Landscape, as the expression of feeling, recalls poem 11, but here there is no rejection of poetic appropriateness as there was at the conclusion of the earlier poem.

47 starts with a rejection of the belief that in death we shall all be absorbed in 'the general Soul' instead of retaining our own identity. Having reassured himself he imagines a divine feast before a final leave-taking ushers in a sublime union with the godhead. The words he uses of this parting are of interest – 'Before the spirits fade away' – because they could also apply to the way images of the after life have appeared, grown, disappeared and reappeared in a trans-formed state throughout the section.

50–58

Both 48 and 49 insist that however light the play of imagination is on the surface of things, deep down sorrow remains. The swallow-flights of song 'dip/Their wings in tears' (48) and 'muffled motions' of sorrow 'blindly drown/The bases of my life in tears.' (49) These dark closures usher in the most troubled section of the whole poem. It is in two parts: a painful recognition of the poet's unworthiness and a ghastly vision of Nature as indifferent to the values people hold so dear.

50 begins with some physical symptoms: his 'light is low', 'the blood creeps', 'the nerves prick/And tingle', 'the heart is sick', and, in an astonishing image that expresses an overwhelming sense of debilitation, 'all the wheels of Being [are] slow.' The poet needs help so five times in 50 and 51 he pleads: 'Be near me'. It is not exactly clear what the symptoms are of, but what does emerge is the poet's acute sense of his own unworthiness. There is a religious intensity reminiscent of some evangelical hymns in his fear that an 'inner vileness that we dread' might be exposed. In 52 his unworthiness includes his verse – 'My words are only words' – and he even goes on to reject the religious confidence of 36 when he says that not even 'the sinless years/That breathed beneath the Syrian blue' – the life of Christ – can keep 'a spirit wholly true/To that ideal which he bears.'

50–52 are so desperately unhappy poems that a reader may feel awkward reading them. 54–56 are similarly painful. They deal with a distraught mind, contemplating a meaningless universe. The significance of these poems will be discussed in section 3.3, so here two general issues will be examined: the relationship between 50–52 and 54–56 and the state of mind the poems express.

The first relation between the personal poems and the nature poems is one of contrast: the desire the poet feels in 52 to be 'wholly true' to an ideal is apparently absent in nature to whom 'The spirit does but mean the breath' (56). Poem 53 establishes a second relation; in the same way in which a man's life might outlive the 'heats of youth' so 'we trust that somehow good/Will be the final goal of ill' (54). At this stage, the relation is no more than a hope, for all the images that crowd in upon the poet – the eternal rubbish heap, the cut worm, the shrivelled moth – suggest that *everything* 'walks with aimless feet'.

The last relation is the most important because it is concerned with the imagery of the poems. The distressed poet thinks in huge, even lurid terms. In the aesthetic sense of the word some of the images in 50–58 are 'sublime'; that is, they are awesome, frightening, mysterious and grand. As we 'climb or fall' the dead 'watch, like God, the rolling hours' (51), and in an impressive development of the idea of life as a difficult climb, the poet is seen as ascending, albeit falteringly, 'the great world's altar-stairs/That slope thro' darkness up to God.' (55). Other images are gothic, even surrealistic: Time is 'a maniac scattering dust' (50), a moth is minutely observed as it is 'shrivell'd in a fruitless fire' (54) and Nature is 'red in tooth and claw' (56). The figure of 'Time' is particularly disturbing; it is a black parody of the sower scattering death instead of life, and it may not be wrong to imagine its manic movements as making it like that mythical creature bent upon destruction – Frankenstein's monster.

The poems about nature show a mind voicing its own anguish in the face of an unfeeling universe. The rhetoric is loud. The poet even imagines nature speaking in a shrill voice – 'With ravine shriek'd against his creed.' (56). And what she has to say is laden with universal doom; words such as 'nothing' and 'all' are readily used – 'I care for nothing, all shall go.' (56) So distressed is the poet that what he says occasionally borders on silliness. The wish to believe 'That nothing walks with aimless feet' (54) is understandable, but who can endorse the hope that 'not one life shall be destroy'd'? It could be that that is a wish that everything is immortal, but if so the confusion between that and death is a sign of the poet's anguish.

There are moments when the poet tries to control what he has been saying by making conclusive statements. In 54 he loudly proclaims 'Behold, we know not anything' in what is surely an attempt to show that his mind has kept a grip on itself in spite of the horrifying images it is encountering. But what a slump in hopes the phrase presents. Readers are summoned to listen by that booming 'Behold', and then what we are given in portentous terms is 'not anything.' 56 closes with another attempt to make sense of his own imaginings. He asks a number of questions, the last one of which is:

> What hope of answer, or redress?
> Behind the veil, behind the veil.

The image of the veil works in a number of ways. It was popular in Victorian religious poetry because, since a veil both reveals and conceals, it could be used to indicate both faith and doubt. Its use here could mean that any hope has been obscured by the terrifying pictures of 'Nature, red in tooth and claw' or that a meaning has been glimpsed. If the latter it might be that the veil is the clue. The veil might remind the reader of a wedding veil, in which case there could be a hint of the prominent Victorian idea that even though the external world makes no sense, comfort can be found in personal relationships.

Tennyson as a poet was interested in extreme mental states. (Remember his family problems.) It looks as if poems 57 and 58 are placed there to draw the reader's attention to just how crazed the poet had been in the preceding ones. In 57 he admits he has been singing (that is, writing) 'wildly' and attempts to bid a more controlled farewell to his friends:

> 'Ave, Ave, Ave,' said,
> 'Adieu, adieu' for evermore.

They are amongst the most poignant and wistful words in the whole poem. The falling cadence, so characteristic of *In Memoriam*, settles so finally on 'for evermore' and the unexpected rhyme 'for'/'more' increases the sadness because its open vowels sound aching and incomplete. Tennyson may once have thought of ending the poem on 57 (an early manuscript indicates this) but probably changed his mind because it is too sad. This is acknowledged in 58 where he talks of 'those sad words' which were like 'echoes in sepulchral halls'. The high Muse, however, enters to promise better closures – 'And thou shalt take a nobler leave.'

59–66

These poems may be read as a continuation of the meditations in 34–38 and 40–48. In those earlier sections the poet reached some assurance about life beyond the grave and came to believe that the dead do remember the living. He is now in a position to approach the subject which is central to the whole poem – love between the living and the dead. These poems, then, are part of a lengthy process of thought, which was interrupted by the anguish of 50–58. It is not surprising, therefore, to find echoes of earlier poems. The first stanza of 59 with its personification of 'Sorrow' recalls 3, and 'dark house' in 60 is an echo of poem 7. Another feature of these poems is worth noting: 59 and 66 serve as 'bookends' in that they are both concerned with other people's reactions to the poet. It could be that by enclosing the meditations on love by these more public poems, there is an implicit recognition that he should see himself in relation to others and not, as he did in 50–58, wallow in his own distress.

The task of writing about love between the living and the dead raises the problem again of what kind of poetic language can adequately express the relationship. The first image he fixed on has his confidence for it is used, in various forms, in 60, 62 and 64. It is that of social class: 60 deals with the 'poor girl', who loves 'one whose rank exceeds her own'; 62 is about a man, who in his youth doted on 'some unworthy heart . . . But lives to wed an equal mind', and 64 explores the lives of two rural boys who grow up together, but who in adulthood lead very different lives – one 'mould[s] a mighty state's decrees' while the other 'ploughs with pain his native lea'. Images drawn from social class are hardly questioned, because, no doubt, they achieve two things: express the gulf between the living and the dead, and do justice to the pain and uncertainty the lesser lover feels when he or she contemplates the greater one. The one doubt about the images concerns whether the greater could think of the lesser. The poet comforts himself in 63 by drawing attention to the pity he feels for the animal creation and concludes that his friend would likewise pity him. 63 is important not only because it buttresses the social class image but because it refers again to the problem of animal pain which had so troubled the poet in 54–56. The fact that he can find it a useful image suggests his mind is more composed than it was.

Tennyson's confidence in the social class image can best be seen in 64. This very popular poem (Bradley said that in *In Memoriam* there were 'none perhaps more exquisitely imagined and written') can be read as a nineteenth-century version of Thomas Gray's 'Elegy', written in 1750, exactly 100 years before the publication of *In Memoriam*. Gray, looking at the graves in a country churchyard, imagined that there lay there men, who might have achieved great things but for the fact of their obscure birth; Tennyson, a century later, pictures a man, who begins in 'low estate' but who rises through his own strenuous efforts (note the punchy alliterations of the second stanza) to 'shape the whisper of the throne'. Yet this man, in repose, 'feels as in a pensive dream, . . . A distant dearness in the hill'. 'Distant dearness' is a beautifully poised paradox: 'distant' suggests the remoteness of the past, and 'dearness' carries the implication that it is close to his heart. But what is never revealed is whether the one to whom the past is both distant and dear ever remembers his former friend – the ploughman. It is the ploughman who closes the poem with this touching question – 'Does my old friend remember me?' What makes that so very touching is that it is the question of both ploughman and poet. It is known that the statesman remembers the hill but not if he recalls his former friend, so the ploughman's question is without an answer for both him and the reader. It is the same with the poet. The whole poem effectively asks – 'Dost thou look back on what hath been' – but neither poet nor reader can answer.

More is offered in these poems than the uncertainty of love. 62 is generous in that the poet hopes that if his friend's remembrance of him causes pain he will be but a 'fading legend of the past'. Poem 65 is of interest in two ways. It is the first happy poem and at its close there is voiced the hope that even the lowly-living might help the high dead:

> Since we deserved the name of friends,
>   And thine effect so lives in me,
>   A part of mine may live in thee
> And move thee on to noble ends.

The words 'noble ends' recall the 'nobler ends' held out as a promise at the close of 58. Other effects making for a quiet confidence are the conclusive impact of 'Since', the reciprocal syntax in the central couplet and the smooth alliterations.

Alliteration is important throughout the section. Listen to the following examples:

> Be sometimes lovely like a bride   (59)

> The little village looks forlorn   (60)

If, in thy second state sublime   (61)

A secret sweetness in the stream   (64)

Those soft, mellifluous alliterations and assonances elevate the tone and lighten the texture of the poetry so it moves with a gentle lilt and something approaching a calm assurance. 60 speaks of the friend as 'a soul of nobler tone'. That could also be a description of some of the poems in this section.

67–72

These poems are notable for the vividness of their imagery and the density of their verbal texture yet, intellectually and emotionally, they are relatively simple, being, with the possible exception of 72, parables of renewal. It is worth asking whether the disparity between the complex language and simple thought is characteristic of *In Memoriam* as a whole, and whether, as some critics believe, this is a fault in Tennyson's poetry. Does his work suffer because its lavish and alluring surface reveals little beneath it, so to speak, but conventional thought and feelings? Or could it be that one of the pleasures of reading Tennyson is the tension between a fertile imagination and an essentially simple mind and heart?

Whatever is made of that problem, it is clear that 67–71 (and possibly 72) try to express one of the central experiences of mankind – the passage from initial illumination, through a period of darkness in which there is no comfort and no assurance of the divine presence and on to a rekindling of the spiritual light that first brightened and warmed the soul. The pattern of experience is one found in the world's spiritual and mystical literature: it is light, darkness, light, or, to adapt other symbols, life, death, life or water, drought, water.

That much is clear. What, however, is difficult is whether the subject is the poet's spiritual growth or his relationship with the friend. A third possibility is whether the latter is just an image or symbol of the former. This is a perpetual problem in *In Memoriam*: it is very often unclear whether religious language is applied to God or to the friend. (I once taught a student who was quite shocked to find that language traditionally applied to Jesus was being used of Arthur Henry Hallam.)

The poems are variously concerned with sleep and dreams. 67 is a night meditation in which the poet in his bed mulls over the significance of the moonlight (often a symbol of poetic inspiration), which falls on his bed and on the 'place of rest' (beds and graves are conventionally associated in poetry) of his friend. But, according to the symbolic pattern of the poem, the light fades – 'the mystic glory swims away' and 'the moonlight dies'. At the close it returns when in the 'dark church . . ./Thy tablet glimmers to the dawn.' A similar pattern is present in 68. The conventional association of sleep and death gives way to the image of the poet dreaming of the time 'When all our path was fresh with dew'. His dream is darkened this time by his fancying that the eye of his friend is troubled, but light is restored when, at the close, he realises that he was only projecting on to his friend his own worry – 'the trouble of my youth'. A significant aspect of this poem is his realisation that dreams can deceive. Because he is aware of this, it is clear that the poet is in control of his experiences, not subject to their frightening changes as he has been in earlier poems.

69 is a very strange poem – a weird, allegorical dream about the poet who is scorned by society because he sings of the dead. His preoccupation with the dead is symbolised by his wearing a 'crown of thorns' instead of bay, the wreath that symbolically adorns a poet's brows. It is an unhappy image, largely because the obvious parallel with Christ confuses the reader. At the close of the poem there is a strange meeting with 'an angel of the night' who 'reach'd the glory of a hand', brought the crown into leaf and uttered words which were not of grief but which, nevertheless, 'were hard to understand.' The kind of reawakening the poet seems to be writing about is a poetic one, but it must be said that the poet has not recently complained of the inability to write.

70 is a surreal, quasi-medieval vision of a city with 'Cloud-towers', 'crowds that stream from yawning doors', and what seem like nightmarish ships – 'Dark bulks that tumble half alive'. This exploration of the obscure passages of the mind – 'shadowy thoroughfares of thought' – ends in a heartening glimpse through 'a lattice on the soul' of 'thy fair face'. 'Lattice' is a very interesting word. In the great Hebrew love poem in *The Bible*, 'The Song of Solomon', the girl's beloved shows himself 'through the lattice'. The parallel reminds us *In Memoriam* is a love poem.

71 does not somuch trace the passage from light, through darkness and back to light as celebrate the light that experience has brought to the poet. Consequently, it is the most triumphant of the group. The vision of the past is almost complete. The opening lines show that he has left behind what threatened him in the early poems – 'death and trance/And madness' – and that he is now 'walking as of old we walk'd'. The contentment is seen in the way that the poem does not develop but rather expands in growing detail the image of the past.

The grammar is of interest. Here are the last three lines:

> The fortress, and the mountain ridge,
> The cataract flashing from the bridge,
> The breaker breaking on the beach.

The sense of a complete picture held firmly in focus is very important in the poem. It is achieved by the absence of verbs – things don't move, they are simply there – and the present participles – 'flashing' and 'breaking' – which suggest that the landscape is eternally present and so not subject to change or decay.

At first, 72 – the poem on the anniversary of the friend's death – seems a contrast. Its thickly textured language (listen to the verbal density of 'With blasts that blow the poplar white') expresses not triumph but the desire to survive a 'disastrous day' that sluggishly climbs to 'thick noon' and touches its 'dull goal of joyless gray'. There are, however, points of similarity with the preceding poems. It is a poem of 'dim dawn . . . issuing out of night' and although it certainly doesn't reach a moment of illumination, its solid strength is more impressive than the numbed or hysterical tones of earlier poems. And at the close there is just the merest hint of light. The day climbs to noon, and though clouds 'drench the morning star' there is this interesting line: 'And sow the sky with flying boughs'. That image is not just concerned with wild, random movement. 'Sow' suggests seeds, which means that the closing words – 'beneath the ground' – point not just to the oblivion of the grave but future growth in the coming season. It is also possible to interpret the poem in terms of the poet. The key to doing this is 'burthen'd brows', a phrase that is surely self-referential. Support for this is found in the fact that the rhyme 'brows/boughs' is also used in 69 when the subject is unequivocally the poet. 72 may be a fall in the poet's spirits but it is not altogether separate from the buoyant parables of renewal.

73–77

These short poems are resigned in tone. In that respect they resemble 72. They are not, however, oppressive. Although 73 opens with balanced phrases that draw attention to the sad falling cadences with which the first line closes – 'So many worlds, so much to do' – it ends with the prospect of a soul exulting in the distant regions beyond death:

> And self-infolds the large results
> Of force that would have forged a name.

'Self-infolds' indicates a soul summoning up and rejoicing in its own formidable strength, and this, along with the fairly aggressive alliterations, creates a tone which is firm if not uplifting.

A number of the poems in this section, including 73, are concerned with fame and time. The subject of fame had been raised in 64, where the social class image had expressed both the gulf between the poet and friend and given a picture of what the friend might have achieved. 73 contemplates 'the head' that 'missed an earthly wreath', yet the poet recognises that, in one of his favourite words, time will make all paths 'dim'. Time is present in 74 and 75; in the former poem the friend is seen in 'likeness to the wise below' and in the latter his present actions elsewhere are imagined as being greeted with 'tumult of acclaim'. In 76 a darker view is taken of the passage of time, and the fame which is called into question is that of the poet. In 75 the poet has acknowledged that his verse gives 'the measure of my grief' while leaving 'thy greatness to be guess'd', so in 76 he contemplates how in 'the secular abyss to come' his work 'shall wither in the vast,/Ere half the lifetime of an oak.'

77 is an interesting poem. It takes up the issue of how time will erode the fame of the poet, but it imagines the circumstances of that neglect in concrete terms. In doing this it has the charm which art displays when it reflects life's everyday trivialities. Things are seen in art, in this case poetry, which are not normally admitted into it – fortuitous, customary objects which are not usually thought of as having the significance we expect in art. The poet imagines what his poems will be used for in the future. They

> May bind a book, may line a box,
> May serve to curl a maiden's locks;
> Or when a thousand moons shall wane
>
> A man upon a stall may find,
> And, passing, turn the page . . .

What fates! His books may be cut up to bind other people's; they may be used, in the way newspaper is used, to line a box or trunk; they may be used as papers by girls who will tie them in their hair each night to form ringlets, and, finally, (the ultimate indignity for a poet?) they will be cursorily glanced at upon a second-hand bookstall. Such details border on the humorous, but he shrugs them off – 'But what of that?' In spite of the oblivion that probably awaits him, the poet steadily expresses his conclusion that

> To breathe my loss is more than fame,
> To utter love more sweet than praise,

78–83

Bradley described 79–89 – the 11 poems that follow the second Christmas poem (78) – as 'occasional' with little connection 'with one another beyond a certain unity of tone', which he characterises as 'calmness'. It's difficult to quarrel with that judgement in general. Here, however, the group will be treated in two sections: 78–83, dealing with reflections that occur to the poet between Christmas and a delayed spring, and 84–89 as a prologue to the poems about the possibility of a mystical union between the poet and his friend.

The Christmas poem invites contrast with 29 and 30. The difference is made clear in the way the last lines of 30 and 78 are paralleled. In the former, Christmas-eve fell 'sadly;' in the latter, it falls 'calmly'. Nevertheless, there is still something sadly mechanical about their celebrations – 'And dance and song and hoodman-blind.' What is obviously missing is 'a token of distress'. The poet then asks the question with which the entire poem started – 'can sorrow wane?' He confirms that it hasn't by appealing to the distinction so popular in this poem (see 4, 5, 16, 19, 48, 49, 52) between depth and surface. Regret's 'deep relations are the same' though on the surface 'her tears are dry.'

It may be that the domestic nature of Christmas prompts the first of these winter thoughts. In 79 the poet comforts his brother. Though he had said 'More than my brothers are to me' in 9, he reassures the one who shared the same landscape and sat at the same knee that he knows 'what force thou art/To hold the costliest love in fee.' What the friend gave him was an 'unlikeness' that 'fitted' the poet's need – 'he was rich where I was poor'.

The connection between 79 and 80 is a loose one. It comes down to this: the contrast between two men is presented in the image of wealth. The poet is surely saying more than that his friend was wealthy whilst he came from a poor home, though in 80 the contrast between the two men is sustained by images that, there, are clearly economic. The poet asks a hypothetical question: what would have happened had the poet died before the friend? The friend becomes a model mourner. He feels a 'grief as deep as life' yet is solidly maintained 'in peace with God and man'. In the 'picture in the brain' the poet forms, the friend 'bears the burthen of the weeks' (the reader might be reminded of 25) 'But turns his burthen into gain.' The next sentence develops the economic image: 'His credit thus shall set me free'. Strange (and inappropriate?) as this image seems, it is not new: poem 1 spoke of 'the far-off interest of tears'. Economics seems too cold and formal a language for the subject of this poem but it may be attractive to Tennyson because it suggests the smooth development (out of sorrow) that his own poem tries but is unable to plot.

81 is also hypothetical, but the imagery is natural rather than economic. Like 80 it recognises the sadness of losing the friend but, unlike some of the earlier poems, it sees something posit-ive – 'sudden frost was sudden gain'. Poems 82 and 83 employ natural imagery, though they put it to different purposes. 82 con-templates with acceptance 'Eternal process moving on', only reserv-ing regrets for the fact that 'Death' 'put our lives so far apart'. 83 is a poem about a delayed spring. In scrupulous detail – 'the foxglove spire', 'speedwell's darling blue' – the poet anticipates spring, add-ing, at the close, that he trusts it will bring lyrical release to him.

It is worth asking what it is that gives these poems what Bradley called 'calmness'. The answer must surely be the confidence with which Tennyson is now handling natural imagery. This is important in the poem as a whole because it shows that two problems with natural imagery are being overcome.

The first is the one touched upon in the discussion of poems 9–21. There a tension was noted between the ease with which natural beauty was evoked and the way in which grief was expressed. Poem 11 implicitly rejected using landscape as a means of expressing grief. In such circumstances it might seem wise to keep the two separate. Something of this attitude survives in 79: don't the stanzas about wood, hill and stream attract for their own sake rather than as pointers to the state of the poet's mind? But in 81–83 things are different; Tennyson once again is able to use the imagery of natural growth to express the inner state of the poet. In 81 natural growth brings about an early harvest, which, in spite of Death's 'sudden frost' was 'sudden gain', because it 'gave all ripeness to the grain'. The poetic language may not be original, but that does not particu-larly matter. What is of importance is that Tennyson uses natural imagery as an analogy of the spiritual life and does so with confi-dence. It is this confidence that breeds 'calmness'.

This is relevant to the second problem. When the poet was distraught the imagery of natural growth was hideously distorted; in 55 the generosity of nature's 'fifty seeds' is not recognised, because the poet obsessively fixes his attention upon the fact that 'She often brings but one to bear.' Consequently, all the poet found about him was husks of seeds – 'chaff'. In 81, however, Death 'returns an answer sweet' – the 'ripeness' of the grain. 'Ripeness' is a popular word in Shakespeare. It may be that Tennyson is deliberately reminding the reader of Shakespeare's deep love for, and celebration of, the natural world in order to show that he no longer looks upon nature as 'red in tooth and claw'.

84–89

These poems are not uniformly happy but they are all confident. This is due to what has been decided in the preceding poems. The poet has established, or feels he has, survival after death, the existence in the dead of memory and an unbroken though transfigured love which the living and the dead can share. He has also established a usage for natural imagery as a metaphoric language for the inner life. All these factors make for a calm and confident tone. In this confidence the poet prepares the reader for one of the major sections of *In Memoriam* – poems 90–95.

84, like 80 and 81, is a hypothetical poem which explores what would have happened had the friend become a member of his family by marriage. (It is important to note that in this section the friend is virtually identical with Hallam.) The poet once again imagines an illustrious public career, but now he adds to that a blissful family life in which the poet, as an uncle, shares. The fact that the children are simply a piece of hypothetical imagining makes the negative of 'I see their unborn faces shine' particularly poignant. The poem is sad, but at its close there is an affirmation of traditional religious language that points to the poet's newly-won confidence. He imagines 'He that died in Holy Land' reaching out his 'shining hand' to welcome them both. It is, of course, important that Christ should offer them his 'hand' as it is an acknowledgement that he is regarded as a friend.

85 is a long poem that looks both backwards and forwards. Its subject is friendship, and its tone is confident. Much that the poet has fought for is taken for granted: after the matter of the friend's death, a death made more delicate by the use of the word so often associated with friendship – 'God's finger touch'd him, and he slept' – there is no difficulty in believing that 'The great Intelligences . . . Received and gave him welcome'. Nor is there any doubt that theirs is a friendship 'which masters Time indeed, and is/Eternal'. Perhaps the most significant expression of confidence is the weight put on the words 'felt' and 'feel'. At the opening the poet forthrightly echoes 27 by asserting 'I felt it, when I sorrow'd most', and when it comes to the difficult matter of the influence of the dead upon the living he states 'I felt and feel'. There are, of course, many objections that can be made against basing belief on something as changeable as feeling, but the

poet doesn't even raise one of them. This was surely a source of comfort to Tennyson's contemporary readers: reading of someone's firm assurance is both necessary and uplifting if one is grieving.

Poem 86 is overwhelmingly positive. It is concerned with the experience of feeling and responding in imagination to an evening breeze (a traditional symbol for poetic inspiration) and a sunset. The stirrings of the heart can be felt in the pulses of the poem's rhythms, which enact the strong, though pleasingly irregular, wafts of a breeze. Consequently, there is little relationship between the rhythms of the word order on the one hand and formal aspects of the poem – its line lengths, rhymes and stanza forms. Its real triumph, however, lies in the unstrained way in which it is both about nature *and* the life of the spirit. In 83 the poet made it clear that nature is used as an analogy for the inner life, but in this poem – the answer to the prayer in 83 that spring will come – there is no division between image and concept: the air that rolls over him is one that passes through 'the dewy-tassell'd wood' and sighs (a word that applies to natural things and people) in him 'the full new life'. To put it in literary terms: the air is not an analogy but a symbol in which many meanings are indivisibly present.

The remaining three poems are not clearly related apart from the way both 87 and 89 are concerned with the friend's speech – the former at Cambridge and the latter at the poet's home. The Cambridge (or College) poem is notable for the way the poet's disappointment at finding idle young men in what had been the friend's rooms (he rhymes 'noise' with 'boys') and the puzzlement over his own feelings – 'The same, but not the same' – gives way to an increasingly vivid and concrete picture of him who had the 'bar [forehead] of Michael Angelo'. Is such praise for a dead friend excessive? 88 is a poem about poetry which uses the image, already present in 21 and possibly hinted at in 83, of the bird. The particular focus of the poem is interesting – it is the difference between poetic intention and actual achievement. The poet intended to 'prelude woe' but, changing the image to that of the classical poet and singer, he admits he 'cannot all command the strings' so

> The glory of the sum of things
> Will flash along the chords and go.

89 is the most idyllic poem yet. At the poet's home away from 'The dust and din and steam of town' (again the tired repetition of 'and') they enjoy 'morning dew . . . mellowing pears . . . the all-golden afternoon . . . the brightening moon' and 'in the distant woods' they

discovered books together while 'the stream beneath us ran' and 'The wine-flask' lay 'couch'd in moss'. But the most important thing is that the friend's voice is heard. 87 was *about* his talk and in 85 there was an imagined dialogue ('or so methinks the dead would say'), but here the living man speaks. All is now prepared for a direct meeting.

90–95

These poems deal with the most important event in *In Memoriam*. Having emerged with the confidences set out in the previous section, the poet now thinks over the possibility of direct contact with the dead, and then with the eagerness of a youthful lover calls upon him to respond. In 95 the friend does.

90 begins with a characteristic feature of the poem – a view which challenges the poet. This particular one is that if the dead were to return they would receive what, in an impressive phrase, Tennyson calls 'An iron welcome'. A rare note of (intentional?) comedy enters: what would happen, for instance, if the dead returned to 'Behold their brides in other hands'? Such comedy lends weight to the sceptical voice, so Tennyson has to work hard to counter it. What he does is shift into another key – that of intimate longing: 'Ah dear, but come thou back to me'. Clearly, this is supposed to be a sufficient answer, for the next poem is indeed a loving invitation to the friend. Three times the poet calls 'Come' at the opening of a stanza and, in keeping with the newly-found confidence in natural imagery, he associates this desired return with spring – 'the sea-blue bird, of March' – and summer with its 'many roses sweet'. The exact nature of the return is not insisted upon: in the second stanza he invites the friend to 'wear the form by which I know/Thy spirit in time', and in the closing stanza he makes this offer: 'Come, beauteous in thine after form'. 92 recognises the objections that could be made to a visible manifestation. In a rare poetic expression of the positivistic spirit of much modern scientific thinking he admits that a 'vision' could just be 'the canker of the brain', and he even goes so far as to point out that a prediction made by the dead may simply be 'spiritual presentiments'.

93 shows that the poet has learnt from the scrutiny of the previous poem. It opens with this terse sentence: 'I shall not see thee.' It then goes on to define a possible relationship. No physical contact is expected, for he believes that 'the Spirit himself, may come/Where all the nerve of sense is numb.' The nature of this relationship is given in a crisp formula of mutual receptivity: 'Spirit to Spirit, Ghost to Ghost.' In the light of this he makes this measured and sonorous appeal:

> Descend, and touch, and enter; hear
> The wish too strong for words to name;
> That in this blindness of the frame
> My Ghost may feel that thine is near.

'Feel' is crucial, and since it is qualified by 'Ghost' there is no contradiction with the earlier line about 'the nerve of sense . . . [being] numb'. Furthermore, the presence of 'blindness' helps the reader to see that the friend might 'touch, and enter', but that the resultant communion would be an entirely spiritual one.

94 is about the state of mind in which the living can receive the dead. The crucial stanza, the third, is about how the spirits of the dead can establish communion:

> They haunt the silence of the breast,
> Imaginations calm and fair,
> The memory like a cloudless air,
> The conscience as a sea at rest

The absence of verbs in the last three lines establishes a peaceful receptiveness that is unstriving and untroubled.

Poem 95, the one in which 'the dead man touch'd me from the past' and 'The living soul was flash'd on mind' is the subject of chapter 5, so readers should turn to it for a more detailed discussion of its significance. For the moment, it is sufficient to note that its second stanza fulfils, in its evocation of the night scene, the conditions set down in 94 for communion between the living and the dead:

> And calm that let the tapers burn
> Unwavering: not a cricket chirr'd:
> The brook alone far-off was heard,
> And on the board the fluttering urn:

The 'calm that let the tapers [candles] burn' is the outward expression of the need for 'Imaginations calm and fair' (94); 'not a cricket chirr'd fulfils the 'silence of the breast' (94) which is necessary for the entry of the departed spirit, and the distant sound of the brook echoes 'The conscience as a sea at rest' (94). The scene then is also a landscape of the mind, a mind that is ready to receive what it most desires – the touch of a dead friend.

96–107

In Memoriam is not the kind of elegy that starts with mourning and ends with glad acceptance because of a particular experience the poet has had. In this respect, as has been said above, it is much closer to ordinary experience, moments of uplift and illumination being followed by unaccountable periods of dullness and even depression. It is a poem with a climax but not a turning point. 95 is that climax, but what follows is a loosely connected group of poems which are subdued in tone. Two of them – 97 and 105 – close with quiet assurance, but some of the others are sad and forlorn. They bear out the truth that mental growth is not a matter of an unhindered, upward movement.

96 is clearly prompted by the occurrence in 95 of 'doubt'. Although the poem wrestles with doubt its stance is robust, the third stanza closing with what has become the honest doubter's creed:

> There lives more faith in honest doubt,
> Believe me, than in half the creeds.

The public rhetoric of those lines (one can hear a preacher's voice in them) expresses both the confidence of the speaker and a strong sense of mission to the wavering. This creed is followed by a single sentence, covering three stanzas, which affirms that he (the friend) who 'fought his doubts' found both 'a stronger faith' and 'Power'. Much of the language deliberately recalls the *Old Testament* accounts of Mount Sinai. The effect of this is to single out the spiritual heroism of the friend.

97 is concerned with faithful devotion. The familiar image of the husband and wife is used to parallel the relationship between poet and friend. It is natural for Tennyson to imagine the wife as the epitome of passive devotion and the husband as a man of the world:

> She knows but matters of the house,
> And he, he knows a thousand things.

It is one of the problems of the poem that the images with which Tennyson seems happiest – class and the lowly status of wives – tend to produce hostility in many of today's readers.

98 is about a marriage that has recently been celebrated. The poet wishes the couple well for their honeymoon journey on the continent. Thinking of their route his mind is led to Vienna (the place of Hallam's death). This makes the tone of the close ambivalent. On the

one hand the poet (here he equals Tennyson) says that he shall never visit that city, and yet he recalls his friend's vivid and spirited account of its busy and varied social life.

99 is also ambivalent. It celebrates the anniversary of the friend's death so the dawn is 'dim', yet by the fourth stanza the breeze has a 'balmy breath', and although it ends with mourning it is a communal bewailing in which the poet is united with all the people who, for whatever reason, keep the day as a memorial.

Poems 100–103 are about moving house. *In Memoriam* is a poem of places – Lincolnshire, London, Cambridge, Vienna, the Severn, the Wye – which are coloured by the memories associated with them. It is memories that make the 'leaving home' poems so sad. 100 is sadly beautiful: the poet climbs a hill and, as in 11, reviews the surrounding landscape – the 'old grange', the 'lonely fold', a stile, a sheepwalk, a quarry – and he reflects that in leaving this place the friend 'once more . . . seems to die.' That is how the poem ends – a very different cadence from 95. The intimate association between feelings and landscape is expressed in 101 by the repetition of 'Unloved' and the presence of other words bearing a negative prefix – 'Unwatch'd' and 'Uncared'. The sadness of this poem is deepened by its proximity to 95, for the garden in which the 'dead man touch'd' him from the past (95) will be left to the 'stranger's child'. The exact nature of the loss is expressed succinctly in 102 by 'Two spirits' – one speaks of how the poet came to know nature and the other of how he shared the landscape with his friend. These two voices rival each other for which is the deepest loss, but at the close 'They mix in one another's arms/To one pure image of regret.' It is a sweet yet painful close – the two embrace each other lovingly but what they unite to present is 'regret'.

103 tempers such regret. It is a strange dream poem in which the imagery of earlier poems – ships and houses – combines and is transformed. The poet travels from a large house and, with a group of maidens, journeys by boat along a river and out to sea, where they meet a ship, which is carrying the friend. The poem ends with a reconciliation which includes the maidens. The sea, particularly in 11, has been questionable, but in this poem it is the scene of an untroubled journey to a rapturous meeting. The inclusion of the maidens is probably symbolic of the place in their friendship of the rest of humanity. The whole poem clearly functions on a symbolic level. A river leading to the sea is a common image of death leading to the larger life beyond.

Poems 104 and 105 are about Christmas in the new home and (a striking contrast) 106 is a stirring New Year call to fight the wrongs of the past. They are clearly related to the poems about leaving home, and it may be that 106 is a summons the poet makes to himself to forget the past and embrace the future. In 104 the poet is a stranger. Bells are tolling, as they did in 28, 'in the mist' and, as before, 'the moon is hid'. The last line – 'But all is new unhallow'd ground' – expresses the feelings of strangeness, but it might also imply that in time it too may be hallowed by significant memories. In 105 the first stanza echoes the previous Christmas poems by ending: 'And strangely falls our Christmas-eve.' Both poems present Christmases that are serious (no games are played), and 105 closes with a quasi-religious promise of new life expressed in the imagery of the seasons. Such a hope is rung out in the 'wild bells' of 106. This (too strident?) poem is a list of wrongs that should be righted. The poet deliberately turns away from private grief to tackle the issues of the day – 'the feud of rich and poor', 'ancient forms of party strife', 'the want, the care, the sin'. The most astonishing rejection is 'the grief that saps the mind'. It is as if the poet is attacking *In Memoriam*!

107 can be read as a sign that the desire to ring out grief has been fulfilled. Though it starts with fierce weather it closes with the domestic comforts of wine, conversation, books and music. The family crowds round 'the great logs' of a fire. The close comes with plurals – 'we/Will drink to him . . . And sing the songs he loved to hear.' The communal has replaced the private.

108–114

These poems are perhaps the most difficult for modern readers. It is not that they are obscure (though 112 is knotty) but that the fulsome praise for the dead is felt to be excessive and, consequently, embarrassing. It is worthwhile asking whether our inability to take high praise seriously is our loss. We do not find it easy to believe in public heroes or people who are masters in many walks of life. It may be that another age will find them more congenial.

The current of thought they follow concerns how sorrow can bring wisdom, and how the friend is the model of the wisdom that we all need. The abandonment of private feeling, advocated in 106, is the subject of the opening of 108. He says 'I will not eat my heart alone' but will share 'sorrow under human skies' in the hope that it 'makes us wise'. The most interesting aspect of the poem is his reasoning. His argument is that if he seeks his own concerns in high or deep matters all he receives in return is his own reflection – 'The reflex of a human face.' That is a form of positivism – since all that can be known is humanity we should give our lives over to understanding our fellow creatures rather than seeking assurances about the transcendent.

Having dedicated himself to finding wisdom he celebrates his friend as the model of what everyone should be. 109 presents a very English notion of human completeness: the friend is not a man of extremes but blends together things that are usually thought to be contradictory. Hence he writes of 'impassion'd logic' and 'manhood fused with female grace.' The praise continues in 110 and 111; the former celebrates the friend's effects upon others, while the latter sees him deserving 'The grand old name of gentleman'. In 112 the poet justifies his disregard of flawed or narrow people because, in comparison, the friend was more complete. The friend's power is evident in an image which was very popular in the nineteenth century – calm and storm. Chaos and disaster were readily spoken of in terms of storm and tempest, so the peace people desired was symbolised by a calm sea. Thus the friend is responsible for 'tracts of calm from tempest made'.

113 repeats the idea that wisdom comes from sorrow and goes on to picture the effect the friend would have had in public life. He is imagined as a politician – 'A potent voice of Parliament' – who, again an image of tempest, was 'A pillar steadfast in the storm' in potentially revolutionary times. From politics the poet turns to knowledge. In 114 knowledge (he probably means of a scientific kind) is seen as dangerous in its tendency 'to burst/All barriers in her onward race/For power', so it must move 'side by side/With wisdom', who is 'heavenly of the soul.' The friend, of course, is the epitome of one 'Who grewest not alone in power/And knowledge' but advanced also 'year and hour/In reverence and in charity.' 'Reverence' echoes the plea in the Prologue for a similar advance in knowledge.

The abandonment of private feeling for public issues is the key to these poems. It is also a useful way of judging them. To many readers Tennyson is much more convincing – more original, more moving – when he is introspective than when he indulges in high sounding public rhetoric. Hence, we are inclined to find the grief and doubt real and the rallying calls bogus. Perhaps we are wrong.

115–124

The poems that close *In Memoriam* don't form a step by step argument but they can be roughly divided into groups: 115–124 have time and change as a common subject matter, and 125–131 sum up the poet's struggles and order his thoughts and feelings in preparation for a reunion beyond death.

115 is the last of the spring poems; it begins: 'Now fades the last long streak of snow'. That line certainly appeals to the eye and ear, but to the reader who is now accustomed to reading Tennyson's

landscapes it has another function: the fading of the snow figuratively points to the fading in the poet of sorrow and regret. Nor would it be wrong to find significance in the natural richness of the scene – violets thickly growing by 'ashen roots', the woodland ringing 'loud and long'; they are surely suggestive of a new and abundant inner life. At the poem's close the analogy between scene and self is explicitly (and unnecessarily) stated – 'and in my breast/Spring wakens too'.

The next two poems introduce the subject of time. The poet in 116 anticipates T. S. Eliot in *The Waste Land* by looking upon April as a time of painful reawakening. He admits that regret is keenlier felt in April but finds that

> the songs, the stirring air,
> The life re-orient out of dust,
> Cry thro' the sense to hearten trust
> In that which made the world so fair.

'Stirring' is often applied to new life emerging from the ground; its use here suggests the whole atmosphere is coming to life. This feeling of things coming to life is more specifically focused in the second line where the resurrection is suggested in 're-orient' (the sun rises in the east and popular belief holds it that Christ will reappear at the end of time in the east) and 'dust' with its associations of death indicates the state from which new life is springing. This sense of new life issues in a new-found trust in natural theology; that is, a trust in the belief that the existence of God can be derived from the character of the universe. This belief, rejected with so much anguish in 54–56, strengthens the confidence with which the poet looks at the world and anticipates the future. A confidence in natural theology may also lie behind 117. Its language clearly echoes the imagery of Jesus' teaching, particularly the parable of the sower, in its belief in time bringing in a 'fuller gain of after bliss'. The language of the parable is most evident in the line: 'Delight a hundredfold accrue'. (In the parable of the sower the seed that fell on good ground brought forth fruit 'an hundredfold', *St Matthew* 13:23.) Tennyson might not be quite formulating an argument about the world and God, but he is drawing on features of the world to awaken and strengthen faith.

118 focuses upon past and future with vivid clarity. In doing this it shakes some of the poet's confidence in natural imagery. That, however, is at the close. The poem starts with the poet grandly summoning us to contemplate the random chances of nature giving way to purpose with the creation of man. The idea is expressed in the

opening two stanzas and then reworked in vivid detail. The 'solid earth' began in 'tracts of fluent heat' and was prey to 'cyclic storms', but with the coming of 'the man', evolution, if that word is not too inaccurate in this context, shows that 'life is not as idle ore' but was forged 'to shape and use.' The imagery is quite complex, but if there is a common thread it is the industrial process. The 'fluent heat' is reminiscent of molten metal and the making of man involves mining, industrial heating and cooling, hammering and, finally, moulding. Tennyson shows himself to be a man of his time in choosing industry as an image of purposefulness. What, or who, is being forged is not clear. The poet talks of 'the man'. That is teasing: is it a representative of mankind or the friend? The poem ends with a summons to 'Move upward . . . And let the ape and tiger die.' In 115 nature was used to express inner feeling; here it stands for the bestial and primitive. *In Memoriam* is a poem that is rarely consistent in its language.

It may be that his assurance about the future allows him to look back. Thus 119 is a parallel to 7. The poet returns to the home of his friend and finds the townscape quite transformed. He 'smells the meadow in the street', hears 'a chirp of birds' and between the houses sees 'A light-blue lane of early dawn'. The radiance of 'light-blue' is a particularly welcome detail in its suggestion of airiness and clarity. Above all there is a mental reunion. In 7 he blankly and despairingly writes of 'A hand that can be clasp'd no more'; 119 closes with these lines:

> And in my thoughts with scarce a sigh
> I take the pressure of thine hand.

120 returns to the topic of 118 – the nature of man. It is of interest because it is a strenuous denial of scientific reductionism, which views man as being merely 'Magnetic mockeries'. The poem bluntly asserts that if that is what science thinks, so much the worse for science. A 'wiser man' (a rare moment of irony) might model himself on Nature – 'the greater ape' – but the poet loudly claims: 'But I was *born* to other things.' The difference between man and the rest of creation is evident in the italicised '*born*': all living things come into being but being *born* implies purpose, particularly when the words that follow are 'to other things.'

121 recalls 95 in that it is a night poem, but whereas in the earlier poem life and death are united, in 121 'Hesper-Phosphor' (Venus, which is both the evening and the morning star) brings together 'my present and my past'. Like many of the nature poems in *In Memo-*

riam the scene is valued for its own beauty and the significances the poet finds in it. A pleasing and quite rare feature is the way it finds material for verse in everyday activities. For instance, this is the penultimate stanza:

> The market boat is on the stream,
>   And voices hail it from the brink;
>   Thou hear'st the village hammer clink,
> And see'st the moving of the team.

The team of horses ploughing is quite conventional and so would be the boat upon the stream had not Tennyson insisted that its purpose is economic. This may colour the line about the blacksmith; the sound of his hammer is heard, but because of the 'market boat' there is an invitation to hear work, trade and industry in the activity rather than just pleasant sounds. The dawn with which the poem ends (the unusual movement from evening to morning is expressive of the poet's buoyant outlook) may prompt the phrase 'While I rose up' in 122. In this poem, a request for a continuing companionship with the friend, there is an echo of 95 in 'As in the former flash of joy' and the familiar strategy of expressing the union of the friends in the natural imagery of 'breeze', 'dew-drop', 'lightning' and 'rose'.

123 returns to the subject of time; it is a very remarkable poem which in an almost visionary way does poetic justice to the thrilling vistas opened up by science. The word 'visionary' is apt because the poet, in his imagination, brings together the past and the present. The contrast between what is and what has been is a popular subject in poetry; here, however, the time-scale is greatly extended so that millions of years are brought together in a single poetic focus:

> There rolls the deep where grew the tree.
>   O earth, what changes hast thou seen!
>   There where the long street roars, hath been
> The stillness of the central sea.

Twice the poet cries 'There'. This makes concrete the changes that have taken millions of years to effect. And even though the past tense is used, the fact that the verb in the second sentence is placed somewhat remotely at the close of the third line has the effect of making the last line as immediate as if it were in the present tense. What happens in the second and third stanzas is of particular interest. The last one is concerned with a retreat into spiritual self-possession and dreaming as a way of holding on to what matters. This is, of course, the reaction (one not unfamiliar in the poem) of someone who recoils from the vision of continual change, and is, thus, in accordance with the tension evident throughout the poem between what nature reveals, and what the poet in the depths of his spirit feels. Nevertheless, the language of the second stanza allays the horrors of vast tracts of time and constant change:

> The hills are shadows, and they flow
>   From form to form, and nothing stands;
>   They melt like mist, the solid lands,
> Like clouds they shape themselves and go.

What may strike the modern reader about these lines is their surprising closeness to the world view of twentieth-century physics – constant change, transformation of form, the insubstantiality of apparently solid matter and even the suggestion in the word 'flow' of the wave theory of matter. It is an astonishing achievement in an age when science was so frequently held to be materialistic in its implications. What is poetically significant about such language is its kinship to spirit. (The reason for this may be its similarity to Biblical language, which speaks of mountains flowing and melting.) Spirits or ghosts are often called 'shadows', 'flow' is suggestive of the kind of metamorphosis that spirits, traditionally, are able to undergo, and 'form to form' is just the kind of language Tennyson uses elsewhere in the poem to express the transformations of the soul beyond death. 123, therefore, presents both the awesome dread and the comforts felt by the poet as he contemplates nature, time and change.

One of the early manuscripts of *In Memoriam* shows that 123 was the last poem. This is of interest because it contains in its last stanza the word 'adieu', which was prominent in an earlier manuscript's closing poem, 57. One can only guess what made Tennyson add more poems. Perhaps 124 was felt to be necessary because whilst it deals very dramatically with the tension between nature and the self it is a louder and more affirmative poem. The manner of 124 is, initially, more logical. It starts with some sweeping (and pretty vague) definitions of God before going on to assert that the poet did not find him in nature. After that negative the poet, through some threatening images – 'an ever breaking shore/That tumbled in the Godless deep' – mounts up to his creed. Significantly, it is one of the popular value words of the poem:

> The heart
> Stood up and answer'd 'I have felt.'

It is a less impressive poem than 123, largely because the implied contrast between head and heart, reason and emotion is so conventional. Still, it has one subtlety often overlooked. Although the poet rejects the view that nature can lead the unaided reason to God, once God has been 'felt' in the heart he can be detected in the natural realm, so the poem closes:

> And out of darkness came the hands
> That reach thro' nature, moulding men.

125–131

This is a section of summaries and references back, although at one point Tennyson introduces yet another image to express the relationship between the living and the dead.

125 and 126 are concerned with love. The former opens with reflections upon verse; the poet admits that there was often 'A contradiction on the tongue.' It is an indication of cultural change that whilst within *In Memoriam* this is felt to be a blemish, the modern reader responds to the ever changing, and even confused, emotional shape of the poem. The poet's justification is that all was done for love, and that in both sadness and strength love was present. The poem closes with an image that recalls 103 – a passage across the seas of death to seek his friend. This image is also an anticipation; poem 131 closes with a very similar one. 126 introduces the new image – that of the lowly subject in a king's court. It is effective because it expresses the gulf between the poet and the beloved and also, in keeping with poems 59–66, allows the possibility of hearing news from a distant place. The poem ends with the poet being comforted by 'a sentinel' (guard) who 'whispers to the worlds of space,/In the deep night, that all is well.' That final phrase is peculiarly comforting. The first woman author in English, the mystic Julian of Norwich, wrote that 'all shall be well', and those solid, earthy monosyllables have echoed through ordinary English speech and literature ('all will be well' appears in *Hamlet*) to express a basic confidence in the ultimate safety and rightness of things.

Poem 127 starts with the phrase and seeks to justify it. Unfortunately, the poem fails. The poet believes that those who know that all is well can remain calm in a tempest:

> Well roars the storm to those that hear
> A deeper voice across the storm.

The trouble is that as the poet explains this basic feeling of safety, what emerges is a distasteful and smug indifference. When everything is in turmoil – 'The red fool-fury of the Seine' piling 'her barricades with dead', 'The fortress crashes from on high', 'the great Æon sinks in blood' – the friend 'O'erlookst the tumult from afar,/And smilest, knowing all is well.' 128 seeks to offer a reason for that confidence. It tries to reconcile the love which survives death with 'the lesser faith/That sees the course of human things.' The point is that faith in the course of human affairs is inadequate unless it is seen as part of a greater whole. The poem closes:

> I see in part
> That all, as in some piece of art,
> Is toil coöperant to an end.

What is combined there is the idea of art as an all-inclusive whole, and history as a purposeful venture. The trouble is that it's vague. The reader might legitimately ask: what end?

The failure of those poems must be due to Tennyson's inability to handle politics and history. He is much happier with the personal notes expressed in poems 129 and 130. He finds he can 'dream his dream of good' when he 'mingle[s] all the world with thee.' The tone of 129 is gentle and intimate and its many polarities – 'known and unknown; human, divine' – are expressive of awe and wonder. The most moving line is the sixth – 'sweet human hand and lips and eye' – in which the poet lovingly dwells on the features that expressed their friendship, moving from contact ('hand'), speech ('lips') to the mute loving look of an 'eye'. In 130 the friend's 'voice is on the rolling air' and he 'standest in the rising sun' and is 'fair' in its setting. Features of previous poems appear to express the poet's love: the friend is felt 'in star and flower', the love for the friend 'involves the love before', and, 'mix'd with God and Nature', the friend is loved 'more and more.' The last stanza opens with an explicitly religious paradox in which the friend is spoken of in the way that God usually is: 'Far off thou art, but ever nigh'. 130 is the apotheosis of the friend and the poet's love for him.

The last poem is a final attempt to blend the public and the private. It does this by deliberately recalling the Prologue. 131 celebrates the human spirit, which, in companionship with God, will bring us 'all we loved'. In the Prologue the poet wrote 'Our wills are ours, . . . to make them thine' and now he writes of 'one that with us works'. He has moved from striving towards God to a view that God actively works with and for humanity in its struggle to lift itself 'from out of dust'. The last line is deeply characteristic of the whole poem – 'And all we flow from, soul in soul.' God, the divine life, is pictured in the subdued image of the sea, and 'soul in soul' is the closest linguistic expression possible of one spirit dwelling in another. Behind it lies the image that has already appeared in *In Memoriam* and which Tennyson will return to in 'Crossing the Bar', the poem that he asked to be printed at the end of all his works. The poet has crossed a sea and is being united with the one he loves.

Epilogue

The Epilogue is the longest poem in *In Memoriam*. Length is important, not because what is said is of particular complexity, but as an expression, an outpouring, of joy in marriage. The poem is a lyrical expression of happiness in which the married couple are central and the friend a special onlooker.

The start is almost comical (and Tennyson is not usually a funny poet) in view of the poem's length; the poet begs 'Demand not thou a marriage lay' but proceeds to offer one because what he once wrote – 'dying songs' of 'a dead regret' – are no longer appropriate from a man whose work is now 'moulded in colossal calm'. In the fifth stanza he sums up his state in words that also apply to the closing stanzas of the poem: 'Regret is dead, but love is more'. In the sixth stanza he calls some of his work 'idle brawling lines'.

These introspective musings upon his own self and his poetry are broken off by the coming of the bride, and what follows (over 80 lines in length) is a delightful picture of the wedding. The charm of these stanzas is generated by the care Tennyson takes in rendering the details of the occasion. After the vagueness of some of the poems, the everyday specificity of the language is invigorating. But, as so often in the poem, such details are not without a figurative function. Two will be examined.

The moment of the marriage sees the bride with

> Her feet, my darling, on the dead;
> Their pensive tablets round her head,
> And the most living words of life
>
> Breathed in her ear.

These words cement the feeling of tradition which helps to sustain all communities. The dead, who were once married on the same spot upon which the bride now stands, are present as silent witnesses as the words that made their and her marriages live are spoken.

Marriages are both made, and made sense of, by the words which solemnise them, hence the Biblical echo of the making of man in the word 'breathed'. This is, in a real sense, a moment of creation. It is also concerned with another kind of creation. In the whole poem the poet's words are life-giving ones and they are spoken in the presence of the dead, not corpses and tablets but the past, his deadened self and, of course, his friend.

The second detail is the signing of the register:

> Now sign your names, which shall be read,
> Mute symbols of a joyful morn,
> By village eyes as yet unborn;

Tradition here is forward looking. There is no sadness in the implication that when future villagers read the names, the bride will be one of the dead memorialised by a 'pensive tablet'. There is, however, an important paradox; although their names are 'mute symbols' they will communicate to the 'unborn' the 'joyful morn' of their marriage. And this reminds the reader of the poet's own writing. Contrary to the fates outlined in 77, the passage carries the hope that the poet's words will be read by 'eyes as yet unborn.' We who read are those eyes.

And so the Epilogue unfolds: the bells, the confetti, the drinking of health and the good wishes. The friend is there and his presence seems quite natural – 'a stiller guest . . . wishing joy'. The couple leave, the family 'range the woods' and 'roam the park' talking and then, unlike the last Christmas, there is feasting, speech-making, singing and dancing till, as in 95, all retire and the poet is left alone to end the poem with his thoughts.

What he offers is a poetic marriage blessing, not unlike the one the fairies bestow at the close of Shakespeare's *A Midsummer Night's Dream*. The moon rises and touches the bridal door. The poet's imagination anticipates the birth of a child, who will be a link between the present generation 'and the crowning race', who 'shall look/On knowledge' and to whom Nature, that has so puzzled the poet, will be 'like an open book'. This 'crowning race' will have nothing in it of the brute and will be like 'the man, that with me trod/This planet'. Thus, the poem is back with the friend – 'That friend of mine who lives in God'. The structure of the long final sentence (it covers eleven stanzas) is episodic, each subject naturally giving way to the next, so it is proper that after the friend comes God, who is finally characterised as the goal of an universal movement:

One God, one law, one element
And one far-off divine event,
To which the whole creation moves.

Why did Tennyson close *In Memoriam* with a marriage? The answer must be that marriages, as at the end of Shakespeare's comedies, carry with them the promise of new life, which will renew the world. Thus, at the close, everything looks forward to the future. Tennyson later said that *In Memoriam* 'begins with a funeral and ends with a marriage – begins with death and ends in promise of a new life – a sort of divine comedy'. The reference to 'a divine comedy' is of interest; Tennyson knew Dante's great poem, *La Divina Commedia*, which explores, in turn, hell, purgatory and paradise. Moreover, there are deliberate parallels such as the bleak townscape of 7 echoing Dante's language about hell. The comparison to *La Divina Commedia* helps the reader to see two closely related things about *In Memoriam*: its sense of purposive movement and the passage from darkness to light and death to life. Both of those things are attempted in Tennyson's poem, though, as has been stressed, neither the movement nor the passage is uniform. Still, to compare one's work with Dante is a huge claim. Readers may ask themselves whether such a claim is too large.

3 THEMES AND ISSUES

3.1 LOVE

In Memoriam is a poem in which the poet struggles to believe that his love for his friend is not rendered meaningless by death. It is not surprising, therefore, that the word 'love' is used a number of times. There are 22 occasions when it functions as a verb and it is used as a noun on 64 occasions. 'Lover' is used once, 'loving' twice and 'loved' 23 times. In addition to those the name 'Arthur' appears 4 times, 'dear' 5 times and 'beloved', 'much-beloved' and 'well-beloved' once each.

That death is bound up with love is the theme of the first and a number of the subsequent poems. What the poet fears is the fading of his affection. A word twice associated with this fear is 'scorn'. In the first poem he fears 'that the victor Hours should scorn/The long result of love' and, in the end, proudly announce their conquest – 'But all he was is overworn.' In 26 the poet longs 'to prove/No lapse of moons can canker Love,/Whatever fickle tongues may say' but if, with the passing of time, love turns to indifference he hopes that death – 'That Shadow waiting with the keys' – will 'shroud me from my proper scorn.' The poet, therefore, sees himself as a knight in a tournament battling against the 'victor Hours' and, given the path image of the poems 22–26, as a traveller (or even a knight-errant) who must be faithful to his beloved until the end. Failure to win or be faithful results in something feared but deserved – 'proper scorn.' That the poet does not, in the end, deserve 'proper scorn' is one of the implicit meanings of the final poems. In 125 love is seen as the motive for all his work, and in 126 it becomes close to a metaphysical principle which guides his life. 130 is the climax. His love has survived; this point is put both negatively – 'I do not therefore love thee less' and positively – 'I seem to love thee more and more.' The triumph of the poem is that his love for his dead friend has not died.

It is possible to read *In Memoriam* in a slightly different way. Even if a reader overlooks the fact that the beloved is dead, the poem can still be read as the expressions of the love of one person for another. This is because the painful questions that press upon the poet are ones that are often asked by lovers. *In Memoriam* asks: will I see him? Does he remember me? Does he still love me?

The fact that the poet voices these touching simplicities of love may, on occasions, make a reader forget that the object of that love is dead. Feelings of longing and the turning over of painful questions, are the common lot of anyone in love, no matter who, or in what state, the beloved is. There are, however, two points that a reader may find problematic: the male beloved and the stress upon physical contact. It must have occurred to many readers whether the love in the poem is a homosexual one. In one sense, of course, it is. The love is between two people of the same gender. The best advice the reader can be given here is to adopt that which W. H. Auden offered about Shakespeare's *Sonnets*: read it as a love poem and don't be put off by masculine pronouns. This, however, doesn't quite resolve the problem. 'Homosexual' has also come to mean the physical expression of love. This clearly raises the issue of the stress on physical contact. The poet's heart 'used to beat/So quickly, waiting for a hand' (7). There is a need for the comforts of physical contact, but, apart from the vague use of 'embrace', such contact is friendly and not erotic. The hand of his dead friend in 7 can be 'clasp'd no more', and in 10 the word is repeated – 'And hands so often clasp'd in mine'. What is important about the language of physical contact is that it brings the reader back to death. The poet longs for contact and yet knows that no contact is possible. The language of touch is, consequently, deeply poignant.

The chief love in *In Memoriam* is for the departed friend, but there is, at least, one other. It is a love rarely stated but frequently implied – the love of Nature. There are three ways in which this is evident: detailed evocations of natural beauty, landscape and memory, and the tension between personal ideals and the laws of Nature. Tennyson does not make the poet in the poem say he loves Nature, but the minute precision with which he sensitively renders the sights and sounds of the natural scene are implicit expressions of love. For instance, consider in 101 the detail of 'the sun-flower, shining fair,/Ray round with flames her disk of seed'. The sound is crisp and precise to the ear, the eye is closely engaged by 'disk of seed', and the flower's name is taken as the basis of an image which in the words 'Ray' (a verb) and 'flames' combines both sun and flower.

In the same poem there is the most eloquent expression of a natural scene being associated with human memory. The poem opens with what seems like a philosophical puzzle:

> Unwatch'd, the garden bough shall sway,
>   The tender blossom flutter down,
>   Unloved, that beech will gather brown,
> This maple burn itself away;

Tennyson offers us an emotional version of the popular philosophical problem as to whether the tree is in the quad when there's no one about to see it. By placing 'Unwatch'd' at the beginning of the line, there appears to be something close to paradox about the fact that the 'bough shall sway'. This paradox is identified in the word 'Unloved'. The point is that it hardly seems possible that these things will carry on when the people who loved them are not there. A landscape exists for Tennyson because it is loved.

This brings together two different kinds of language: the personal and the natural or scientific. It is the relationship between these two that is challenged in 54–56. When the poet asks in 55: 'Are God and Nature then at strife?' he is identifying God with personal qualities such as concern or pity, and Nature as an unfeeling process, which could be accurately and coldly described by the naturalist or scientist. The pain for the poet is that the two languages seem to have nothing to do with each other. Hence the anguish in 56 of man 'Who trusted God was love indeed/And love Creations's final law'. The struggle of *In Memoriam* is to be able to say that it is, to affirm that personal language can be applied to the course of Nature.

There is one other aspect of love that needs to be mentioned: its relationship with poetry. Two aspects will be looked at: the imagery of the poem and the desire to express love in poetry. The poem abounds in images of love and marriage. There is, for instance, the ballad-like tale in 8 of 'A happy lover', and in 6 a number of stories – about parents and children and lovers – are used to illustrate love and sudden loss. Another tale (*In Memoriam* is a poem of miniature stories and ballads) is the sad one in 60 of the girl of low birth who loves the upper-class young man. On several occasions – 9, 13, 17, 40, 85 – the poet speaks of himself as a 'widower' or as 'widow'd'. There are several mentions of marriage – 40, 59, 62, 84, 98 and the Epilogue.

But *In Memoriam* does not merely use images related to love, it sees poetry as a means of expressing love. In 21 the poet says: 'I do but sing because I must', where 'must' is an inner compulsion best understood as love. The purpose of verse is more explicitly stated in 77: 'To utter love [is] more sweet than praise.' In the third stanza of 125 love is seen to be present breathing through care and setting his seal upon whatever is 'sweet and strong'.

3.2 THE POET'S PREOCCUPATION WITH THE ART OF POETRY

It is not mere critical convention to call the voice in the poem 'the poet'. One of the most important aspects of *In Memoriam* is its reflexive character; that is to say, the poet's writing of poetry becomes a subject of the poem. This is the case in the following: Prologue, 5, 8, 16, 19–21, 23, 37, 38, 48–49, 52, 57–58, 65, 75–77, 83, 88, 106, 125 and Epilogue. What picture of poetry emerges from these?

It is certainly not a simple one. There is a tendency in some critics to see a development (though not necessarily a smooth one) from poetry as private self-expression to public responsibility. E. D. H. Johnson, for example, views the poem this way, defining four stages: poetry as release, as escape, as self-realisation and as mission. (The essay can be found in the *In Memoriam* Casebook edited by John Dixon Hunt.) That is far too schematic for *In Memoriam*; what is moving about the poet's interest in poetry is its fragmentary and unsystematic character. It is not so much a question of progress as new thoughts and repeated ideas coexisting in a bitty and yet convincing way. For instance, the idea that poetry eases pain appears in 5 where it is said to be a 'sad mechanic exercise,/Like dull narcotics, numbing pain.' But this idea is repeated in 75: 'I leave thy praises unexpress'd/In verse that brings myself relief'. And in both poems another concern is voiced – the inadequacy of verse to express either real grief or the worth of the friend.

The need to express oneself is sharply felt in the poem, but the poet cannot always achieve lyrical release. This is the subject of 19 in which the rhythm of the tide in the Severn and the Wye is used as an emblem, or even an allegory, of poetic expression: when the tide is full there is 'silence in the hills' and the poet is 'fill'd with tears that cannot fall', but when 'The tide flows down, the wave again/Is vocal' and his 'deeper anguish also falls' so he 'can speak a little then.' The poem works by inviting the reader to see the differences between rivers and the poet; the river will regularly fill and empty the Wye Valley, but moments of lyrical release will probably only come occasionally to the poet and then, as in the cast of this one, he still may only be able to express himself 'a little'.

The moment of lyrical release, a moment central in Romantic and post-Romantic verse, is often embodied in the imagery of the gliding movement or the songs of a bird – is not John Keat's 'Ode to a Nightingale' a meditation on the elusive yet elevating power of the poetic imagination? Tennyson handles the image with remarkable ease: just as the bird mounts, circles, dips and pours forth song, so the poet's imagination aspires to a lyrical outburst. In 21 the poet says he must 'pipe but as the linnets sing'; in 48 lyrical verse is seen as something unable to 'part and prove' but is valued as 'Short swallow-flights of song, that dip/Their wings in tears, and skim away', and in 88 the bird becomes an ideal poet, who, unlike the one in the poem, can express with ease the extremes of grief and joy: 'And in the midmost heart of grief/Thy passion clasps a secret joy:' It is interesting to note that poetic success is expressed in the language of that physical contact for which the poet so longs – 'clasps'.

But release is a different matter from worth. A question that haunts the poem is the value of what the poet has done. The failure of poetry to express either grief or the true worth of the dead friend has already been touched upon. There are also external critics. In 21 unsympathetic listeners dismiss the poet's outpourings as weakness, the parading of feeling or sheer irresponsibility in the face of climactic public events. In 37 the critical voice of Urania, the muse of Heavenly poetry, is heard dismissing his work, and in 76 and 77 he anticipates the indifference with which his work will be met in the future. The hardest criticism, though, is that which he offers himself. The Prologue ends with this plea: 'Forgive these wild and wandering cries', and in the Epilogue he writes of

> the songs I made
> As echoes out of weaker times,
> As half but idle brawling rhymes,
> The sport of random sun and shade.

The word 'brawling' may deliberately recall Mariana, an abandoned woman, who, in Shakespeare's *Measure for Measure*, a play Tennyson knew quite well, spoke of 'my brawling discontent'. Given that Mariana is a woman forsaken by her lover, the implication may even be that the poet stigmatises his verse as merely the bitter expression of a rejected lover.

At times doubt about the value of the verse is oddly akin to some present-day theories of literature that stress the limits of language and see many works as simultaneously building and demolishing meanings. But whatever causes modern doubt can't be responsible for the self-questioning of *In Memoriam*. A possible answer, though, is an awareness that the poetry stands in an ambiguous relationship to the consolations offered by religion. There are moments in the poem when the poet seems to admit that he ought to have found comfort in faith rather than indulging in self-expression. The difficult 37 can be read in this way. The muse of Heavenly poetry scorns him and the tragic muse (Melpomene) can offer little 'To lull with song an aching heart', and the poem closes in a remarkably obscure way with the suggestion that he 'loiter'd in the master's field/And darken'd sancti-ties with song.' Can that be read as the poet recognising that although he 'loiter'd in the master's field' (a reference, surely to Christ) all he did was darken the sanctities of faith with his verse? Since the impossibility of religious verse is often the subject of that verse, it may be that the poet is recognising that in choosing to express himself he has obscured the light of faith. An uneasy attitude to religion is also evident in 52, when, in justification for his 'plaintive song' ('song' means poem) it is said that not even the life of Christ – 'the sinless years/That breathed beneath the Syrian blue' – can keep 'a spirit wholly true/To that ideal which he bears?'

The uneasy relationship between poetry and religion may be the result of the deeply personal inspiration of the poem. The greatest hope that the poet has is not a conventionally religious one but the hope that his work might please the friend. In 38 the poet imagines that his words are heard:

> If any care for what is here
>   Survive in spirits render'd free,
>   Then are these songs I sing of thee
> Not all ungrateful to thine ear.

In 65, the first happy poem in *In Memoriam*, he actually dares to hope that his verse might 'move thee on to noble ends.' There is, surely, a richness of meaning in 'move': the dead friend will be both emotionally moved and also inpired to progress to finer things. The fact that the poet can't think of a better end for his own verse may lie behind the dissatisfaction with verse and the uneasy relationship his poetry has with religion.

3.3 SCIENCE AND RELIGIOUS FAITH

The angry critic in 21 makes this accusation against the poet's preoccupation with his grief:

> 'A time to sicken and to swoon,
>   When Science reaches forth her arms
>   To feel from world to world, and charms
> Her secret from the latest moon?'

The point is clear: this is no time to dwell on private grief when science is achieving so much. Indeed, there is a note of surprise in the voice, for since science herself is alluring – 'reaches forth her arms/ To feel . . . and charms' – it is inconceivable that anyone would want to ignore her.

And Tennyson does not. There are two reasons for this. The first is that for all its privacy, the poem is not merely introspective; Tennyson does heed the view of the imaginary critic and writes about what concerns his fellow human beings. The second reason is the one that relates the findings of science to religious faith. It has been stressed in Section 3.1 that the poet in the poem wants to believe that personal values such as love and compassion are of supreme importance. The traditional expression of this belief is a religious one: God is good, and his goodness is evident in the world he has made. But in the nineteenth century science seemed to erode this view. Increasingly the picture of the world it revealed was an aimless, indifferent and even cruel one. Such aimlessness was most evident in the death of the friend. In thinking about him, the issues of the apparent conflict between science and religion emerge.

It is helpful to understand in more detail how science challenged religious faith. There are two quite closely related reasons. The first is the question of time. The change from a short to a very long time-scale is one of the biggest mental adjustments people in the West have made in the last 150 years. Tennyson was born into a world in which nearly everybody believed in a time-scale deduced from the Bible. The dates given in *The Old Testament* (the calculations were done in the seventeenth century by Archbishop Ussher) revealed that the world had been created in 4004 B.C. It is important to imagine what it must have been like to believe that. The world was less than 6000 years old, and if one regards 70 years as the normal human life-span then each life represents a significant proportion of the entire stretch of the world's history. Such figures allowed the possibility of feeling both secure and important. But even before

Tennyson was born, doubt was being cast on this. James Hutton concluded his *Theory of the Earth* (read as a lecture in 1785 and published in 1795) with these ominous words: 'The result, therefore, of our present inquiry is that we find no vestige of a beginning – no prospect of an end.' The real assault upon the old time-scale began in Tennyson's youth; Charles Lyell's *Principles of Geology* (1830) and Robert Chambers's *Vestiges of Creation* (1844) were just two of many books that pointed to a staggeringly immense time-scale for the universe, thereby implicitly raising the question: what significance can people have if they exist for such a short period of time? But science revealed something even more frightening: not only was the world old, it was also the result of very many changes, some catastrophic and others gradual. The hills that people saw were not therefore, those that Adam saw on the first day of creation but eroded stumps left by eruptions and erosion. When sensitive people contemplated an immense time-scale and the instability of the world they very probably experienced spiritual vertigo.

The second reason for a conflict between science and religion was the impact of biology and geology. In the eighteenth and early nineteenth centuries there was much respect (both intellectual and popular) for what is called the argument from design. This was an argument for the existence of God which sought to show that evidence of design or organisation in the natural world pointed to a supreme designer, namely God. The most popular formulation of this argument was made in 1809 by William Paley – if a watch required a watch-maker, did not an eye require an eye-maker? It was a bold, comforting and pleasingly commonsensical argument because it embraced the whole universe, instilled a feeling that everything was providentially designed by a good God, and appealed to the very basic idea that things look as if they've been made by someone. Perhaps the most attractive aspect of the argument was that its starting point was familiar details of the natural world – a leaf, a wing, a flower, an eye – which pointed to the existence of a great, wise and good designer.

It is possible to read much nineteenth (and a great deal of twentieth) century literature as a response to what happens when people lose faith in this argument. The influences of biology and geology were mainly responsible for that loss. They both examined how change, growth and transformation took place in the world, and showed that these things can be accounted for in naturalistic terms. Things might look as if they've been designed but, in fact, they've just grown, in their own way, to be like that. Strictly speaking, the two approaches are not incompatible, but the effect of much scientific work was to render the hypothesis of God unnecessary in many people's minds. But there was an even more disturbing effect. The picture of the world which biological and geological studies produced was neither that of the argument from design nor that which is associated with the popular term 'Mother Nature'. The world was neither benign nor caring. Thousands of species had been scrapped in the march of time (this was the lesson of the fossils), and the actual process by which species grew and survived was savage and ruthless. The world was, at its best, neutral and impersonal, and, at its worst, positively hostile to all those personal values – love, pity, kindness, duty, compassion – which people believed in and tried to govern their lives by.

It is evident that the two factors – the lengthening of the time-scale and the effects of biology and geology – combined in people's minds to produce the image of a vast, blind world system which, in its violent struggle for survival and change, cares nothing for all that people most value. One does indeed wonder why the critic quoted at the beginning of the section spoke of science charming her secrets, when the picture it evoked was neither magical nor alluring.

In *In Memoriam* time and biology and geology are not treated separately, nor does Tennyson explicitly raise the issue of science and religion. There are, nevertheless, a few poems which are preoccupied with time. Two deserve particular attention – 118 and 123. What makes the attitude to time in these poems interesting is the way it is poised between fear and fascination. Time is awesome and even frightening yet its vast (an important word in the poem) tracts stimulate the imagination. 118 begins with both fascination and fear:

> Contemplate all this work of Time,
> The giant labouring in his youth:
> Nor dream of human love and truth,
> As dying Nature's earth and lime.

Time is something to 'contemplate' (a spiritually-elevated word); it is something sublime and awesome – 'The giant labouring in his youth'; but there is an implicit fear that the materials with which Time works – 'earth and lime' – are all that people are made of. Time is an object of wonder but not if human beings are nothing but chemical substances which will die with Nature. A similar kind of exciting unease is evident later. A sentence which runs on from one stanza to another appeals to what 'they' – the geologists – say:

                                        They say,
         The solid earth whereon we tread

               In tracts of fluent heat began,
                 And grew to seeming-random forms,
                 The seeming prey of cyclic storms,
               Till at the last arose the man;

The juxtaposition of the palpable 'solid earth' with the insubstantial
'tracts of fluent heat' is invigorating in its promise to reveal a
fundamental reality very much at odds with, to use a word repeated
in the stanza, 'seeming'. But for all the heady sense of adventure (the
adventure is also a poetic one because Tennyson has to find a
language adequate to this fascinating object) there is the threat of
chaos; the forms (a word which in this poem implies something firm
and fixed) are 'random', and the earth is, like a vulnerable creature,
'a prey of cyclic storms'. Yet there is relief in the stability provided by
the steadying definite articles in 'Till at the last arose the man'.
   In 123 the tension between fascination and fear is less evident, but
is, nevertheless, there in the way the last stanza retreats into
introspection – 'in my spirit will I dwell' – after the first two have
been concerned with the thrill of time and change. The first opens by
way of a contrast between the past and the present:

               There rolls the deep where grew the tree.
               O earth, what changes hast thou seen!
               There where the long street roars, hath been
               The stillness of the central sea.

The idea of change wrought by time is evident in the contrasts; it's not
just a case of sea and land, but of the moving water – 'rolls' – and the
fixed tree, and the 'roar' of the street as opposed to the 'stillness' of
the sea. The last contrast is a particularly inviting one for 'roar' is
conventionally applied to the sea (there are many such applications in
Tennyson's verse) and 'central' is a word often used of cities. Perhaps
the most exciting aspect of this poetic language is that though it was
formed to express the picture of the world disclosed by science it is
like other imagery in the poem in that it can be read as expressive of
the poet's concern for his friend. In 119 the poet has returned to the
street where his friend lived, so a reader might readily associate the
streets of 119 and 123. If so, the landscape and townscape could be
expressive (as in 7 and 119) of a mind which has moved from a wild

'roar' to a 'stillness'; conversely, though, 'stillness' might remind a reader of death as in 'Hath still'd the life that beat from thee.' (6)

54–56 tackle the problems created by the new time-scale, biology and geology. The reader should always remember the strident, rhetorical tones of these poems and the way 57 and 58 attempt to allay their shrill anxiety. This, however, should not obscure the fact that the poet is struggling with large and important questions. 54 opens with a desperate hope – 'Oh yet we trust that somehow good/Will be the final goal of ill'. There is something very moving about the hopeless vagueness of 'somehow'. His yearning is to believe that 'nothing walks with aimless feet', an image which is particularly sensitive since it was used of the companionship he shared with his friend. What is cruelly evident in a number of sharply focused images is that things do appear to be aimless – the cut worm, the shrivelled moth. Hence the desperation of

> I can but trust that good shall fall
> At last – far off – at last, to all,
> And every winter change to spring.

The second line expresses the hope of a final resolution, but its very structure – repetitions and qualifications – weakens the possibility and pushes it so far into the future that it seems synonymous with a never, never land.

55 is more collected. It asks whether our wish that 'No life may fail beyond the grave' derives from 'The likest God within the soul?' In other words, God is identified with personal qualities of love and pity. The poet then bluntly puts the problem:

> Are God and Nature then at strife,
> That Nature lends such evil dreams?

Nature only seems to be concerned with 'the type' (the species) and not 'the single life' – 'of fifty seeds/She often brings but one to bear.' That's the picture biology gives of 'Mother Nature.' Death is far more common than life, so at the end of the poem the poet stretches 'lame hands of faith' and simply gathers 'dust and chaff'; dust, of course, means death as in 'ashes to ashes, dust to dust', and chaff is the husks of the seeds which were not brought to bear.

In 56, however, both biology and geology conspire against the belief that Nature is concerned with types:

> From scarped cliff and quarried stone
> She cries, 'A thousand types are gone:
> I care for nothing, all shall go.'

What emerges from the 'scarped cliff and quarried stone' are fossils which show that thousands of types have disappeared. The hardest question to ask is whether man will go the same way. Man struggles to believe that 'God was love indeed/And love Creation's final Law', and this in spite of 'Nature red in tooth and claw'. That last phrase has passed into the common language so it is not easy to recognise just how frighteningly impressive it is. Nature either remains something hidden from us or is something just too terrible to look at. Hence, we don't see how creatures tear each other, we just see, as it were, the beast itself emerging with blood on its fangs and talons. If man's fate is just to be 'seal'd within the iron hills' (become just another fossil) the violence of 'Dragons of the prime' (dinosaurs)is preferable, presumably because nothing noble was expected of them.

124 offers a resolution of this terrible conflict. In vague though comprehensive terms he evokes the divine – 'He, They, One, All' – and then announces his rejection of the argument from design:

> I found Him not in world or sun,
> Or eagle's wing, or insect's eye.

The negative is weightily rendered by the delay'd 'not' and the fact that the first four words bear an emphatic stress; and what is denied is Paley – the 'insect's eye' surely refers to the eye/eyemaker argument. If the poet never found 'Him' in nature the horrors of 54–56 are not so undermining. The positive assertion is, unsurprisingly, a quasi-mystical one in that, as elsewhere in the poem, all the weight is placed on the word 'felt':

> A warmth within the breast would melt
> The freezing reason's colder part,
> And like a man in wrath the heart
> Stood up and answer'd 'I have felt.'

As well as the conventional opposition of head and heart, Tennyson employs subdued religious language. 'A warmth within' is reminiscent of John Wesley's description of his conversion – 'I felt my heart strangely warmed' – and the assertion is in the form of an evangelical testimony; the heart 'Stood up' and appealed to personal experience – 'I have felt'.

3.4 CIRCULAR MOVEMENT AND THE IDEA OF PROGRESS

Some modern critics are fascinated by circles. They delight in showing that writers have a cylical (moving in circles) rather than a linear (moving in a line) idea of time and history. *In Memoriam* has, consequently, been interpreted as an essentially circular poem. There is some justification for this.

A circle is a traditional symbol for perfection, so when the poet wishes to imagine an ideal life an image of circular movement seems appropriate – 'And orb into the perfect star' (24). A circle, also, protects what is within it from the outside (see section 4.1 on the stanza form). Hence the poems about the return of the friend's body have a number of circular images, expressive, no doubt, of the care and concern the poet has for his friend's body. In 12 his imagination, expressed in the image of a bird, passes over 'ocean-mirrors rounded large' to the boat:

> And circle moaning in the air:
> 'Is this the end? Is this the end?'

And in 17 there is some comfort in the way he imagines the boat moving 'Thro' circles of the bounding sky'. The most prominent example of circular movement is, of course, the seasons. In so far as the poem is plotted round Christmas and spring poems it may be said to be circular in its design. In the 'path poems' (22–26)the sense of a perfect life is expressed in the circular movement of the season – 'And glad at heart from May to May' (22). A final attraction of circular imagery is that it does justice to the poet's aspiration – to recover the gladness of the past – as well to the reader's sense that the poet's grief is never quite appeased. A number of poems (100 is an example) return, as in a circle, to the foundation experience of the poem – the death of his friend.

But it won't do to concentrate on circles alone. Not only are some of the arguments frail (is the design of the poem really circular?), they ignore the presence of the Idea of Progress. Consider the Prologue with its wish that 'knowledge grow from more to more'. The submerged image is of something either accumulating or branching out. Even more striking is poem 1. There is the image of upward movement – 'men may rise on stepping-stones', and linear movement stands behind the second stanza:

> But who shall so forecast the years
> And find in loss a gain to match?
> Or reach a hand thro' time to catch
> The far-off interest of tears?

It is difficult to 'forecast' what will happen, but the possibility of doing so depends upon a linear notion of time, and even though the juxtaposition of 'loss' and 'gain' seems too neat, it is qualified by the second image of reaching 'a hand thro' time' to secure 'The far-off interest of tears'. That is a strange image – the economics of mourning. The tears we shed now will, as in a savings account or stocks and shares, grow with the passage of time to produce a substantial benefit for the mourner. In the Epilogue the forward moving nature of the poem is evident in the subject (marriage is an occasion for looking forward), the hope that the next generation will be 'a closer link/Betwixt us and the crowning race' and the final image of God as the 'one far-off divine event,/To which the whole creation moves.' Those who doubt that the idea of Progress is important should observe that the very last word of the poem is one of motion – 'moves.'

Images of Progress, growth and forward movement are not only present at the opening and close of the poem. Expectation is the subject of the ballad of 'A happy lover' (8). In 9 and 17 the poet writes: 'Till all my widow'd race be run'. In the grief of 18 the poet recognises that his life 'slowly forms the firmer mind', and in 22–26 (and elsewhere)the dominant image is that of the path of life. Even natural images which are so frequently seen as circular can be read as expressing forward movement. In 26 the poet sees 'within the green the moulder'd tree', and in 54 he desperately hopes that 'every winter [will] change to spring.' Another image of movement that, significantly, is employed in these grim poems about nature is a basically architectural one in 55 – 'the world's great altar-stairs/That slope thro' darkness up to God.' Elsewhere nature provides the idea of progress. In 118 man 'arose . . . throve and branch'd from clime to clime,/The herald of a higher race'. The bold conclusion the poet makes is that we should 'Move upward . . . And let the ape and tiger die.' It is interesting to note that in the previous poem, 117, the growth of crops was expressed in an image of growth towards a fruitful future. His hope for 'fuller gain of after bliss' is given in an image drawn from the parable of the sower in which the seed on good ground yields 'a hundredfold'.

When reading *In Memoriam*, it is important to recognise both the circular and the linear movements. In doing this, the reader will want to ask which is the more important and what relation they have to the grief which is the origin of the poem.

4 TECHNIQUES

4.1 STANZA FORM

The grief and uncertainty of *In Memoriam* are expressed in, and created by, its simple yet flexible form, a quatrain (a four line stanza) consisting of a couplet and an enclosing rhyme – ABBA. Two principal effects are made possible by this form. The first is that the thoughts and feelings of the poet are protected by the enclosing rhyme; that is to say, the need for consolation is enacted in the very structure of the verse in its isolation of what is private and introspective. This is evident in the last stanza of 5, which is a meditation upon the soothing effects of verse and also a self-referential comment upon the function of the stanza form:

> In words, like weeds, I'll wrap me o'er,
>   Like coarsest clothes against the cold:
>   But that large grief which these enfold
> Is given in outline and no more.

The enclosing rhyme does 'wrap' itself around the central couplet like clothes ('weeds') so that the words do 'enfold' that 'large grief', and as the shape of the stanza becomes clear in the last line, the 'outline' (a pun on out or outer line) of an intensely private emotion begins to emerge.

The second effect derives from the remoteness of the final rhyme. Because of the pithy, concentrated, self-affirming nature of the couplet, the final rhyme sounds weaker, and thus whatever is said at the close sounds much less assured. Instead, then, of the firm resolution so often associated with rhymed poetic closure, the final line often sounds like a weak, attenuated echo. This weakening is movingly present in the last stanza of the self-questioning 16:

> And made me that delirious man
> Whose fancy fuses old and new,
> And flashes into false and true,
> And mingles all without a plan?

The word 'plan' with its obvious meaning of intended design ought to close the poem on a resolved note, but the remoteness of the rhyme and the negative – '*without* a plan' – enact the puzzled confusion of someone reeling from a shock, who is aware that there might have been order ('plan') in his life but recognises that, like the 'unhappy bark' earlier in the poem, he merely 'staggers blindly'.

It is, of course, mistaken to expect that both of these possible effects are present in every stanza. Also mistaken is the view that they are the *only* effects. There are four others, two of them concomitants and two variants, that, though minor, make important local contributions to the poem.

First, there is the capacity of the enclosed couplet to express what is most private and most important. An example is the desire for reciprocal indwelling, which is expressed with great longing in 65:

> And thine effect so lives in me,
> A part of mine may live in thee

The force of that couplet depends on more than the end rhyme; its virtual repetition of syntax, its internal rhymes (thine/mine), and its alliterations, all give it a compressed and intense feeling, which is expressive of its importance to the poet.

The second concomitant is, to refer back to section 3.4, that the stanza can have a circular quality. This is the first stanza of 31:

> When Lazarus left his charnel-cave,
> And home to Mary's house return'd,
> Was this demanded – if he yearn'd
> To hear her weeping by his grave?

Of course, the stanza progresses from a return to a question, but if the words of the enclosing rhyme are attended to, it is seen that they both have the same meaning – 'charnel-cave' is equivalent to 'grave'.

The first variant is the way Tennyson sometimes extends his syntax over stanzas, thereby allaying to a certain extent the enclosed character of the form. This occurs in the uncomfortable Christmas poem, 105, in which the poet regards celebration as unfitting, largely because the family has moved. Instead of 'harp', 'flute' and 'dance' he looks to the hope of new life in the cycle of nature, a hope he expresses by running the penultimate stanza into the final one:

> save alone
> What lightens in the lucid east
>
> Of rising worlds by yonder wood.

The word 'east' is associated with the sun, so in the run-on stanza 'rising' seals that association and mimes the new life it brings by the fact that there has been an unbroken progress in meaning across the stanzas.

The second variant is a deliberate paralleling of the first two and the last two lines, which dilutes the strength of the central couplet. In 16 the third stanza (which also runs into the fourth) functions in parallel images:

> That holds the shadow of a lark
> Hung in the shadow of a heaven?
> Or has the shock, so harshly given,
> Confused me like the unhappy bark

In that stanza the contrast in images, the first of the skylark and the second of the sea, is enforced by the fact that the first two lines form a question (always an emphatic way of closing a line) while the next two begin another.

4.2 THE UNITY OF THE POEM

The unity of a work of art is an issue related to, but distinct from, its design. Chapter 2 made it clear that although there are sequences within *In Memoriam*, the poem forms neither a continuous narrative nor a systematic argument. Yet a poem can meander, moving by chance associations of idea or image, and still have a unity. This is the case with *In Memoriam*. Clearly the presence of a thinking, feeling and speaking self-expressing grief, asking questions, remembering events and making statements is a unifying factor. Furthermore, there is the use of a single stanza form, and the important subjects dealt with in chapter 3. To those can be added the preoccupation with dreams and seasonal change. In addition, there are four other things that help to establish a unity.

The first is closely related to the themes of the poem. In *In Memoriam* there are a number of recurring images. There is for instance, the tension between music and discord. In the Prologue there is an aspiration made more climactic by the run-on stanza, that harmonious working of the mind and soul 'May make one music as before,/But vaster.' In contrast to the desire for harmony is the fear of discord. In 56 both images appear in a stanza about man's contradictory state:

> A monster, then, a dream,
> A discord, Dragons of the prime,
> That tare each other in their slime,
> Were mellow music match'd with him.

There is a similar tension between purposeful and purposeless movement. The sequence of poems 22–26 starts with a golden memory of 'The path . . . which led by tracts that pleased us well' but closes with: 'Still onward winds the dreary way'. In 4 there is the image of 'a helmless bark', whilst in 125 the quest over the sea of death to a reunion is purposeful: 'till I sail/To seek thee on the mystic deeps'. Some images don't stand in sharp contrast with others. In 7 and 8 the house is central and in 6 and 20 the family. In 89 the happiness of the family is expressed by the image of perfection – the circle: 'O bliss, when all in circle drawn/About him, heart and ear were fed'. Although the images of house and family don't usually stand in a formal contrast to others, there are occasions when they do. In 20 the children mourning the death of their father are presented as sitting by an empty grate – 'For by the hearth the children sit/Cold in that atmosphere of Death' – whereas in 107 there is this image of domestic happiness which echoes Shakespeare's 'And Tom bears logs into the hall':

> Bring in great logs and let them lie,
> To make a solid core of heat;
> Be cheerful-minded, talk and treat
> Of all things ev'n as he were by;

Closely related to the unifying role of imagery are linked or contrasted pairs which, by making the reader aware of earlier poems, plot changes in mood. There are two poems about the Yew tree (2, 39), two which personify 'Sorrow' as female (3, 59) and two on the friend's house (7, 119). Change in mood is very conspicuous in the last pair; the desolate urban townscape of 7 expresses the utter absence of the friend, and the symbolism of the dawn is reversed to make it signify blankness instead of new life, whereas in 119 the country is present in the city ('I smell the meadow in the street') and, most important of all, the poet says, in the present tense: 'And in my thoughts with scarce a sigh/I take the pressure of thine hand.' Poems 11 and 15 contrast calm and storm, 18 and 67 are about the friend's grave, and 130 answers the fears of 1 and 26 that the poet's love might die.

A third unifying element is the recurrence of individual words. The prevailing tone of at least the earlier part of the poem is partly established by the repetition of 'dark' (7 times), 'darken' (once), 'darkening' (once), 'darken'd' (twice) and 'darkness (14 times). Those words are associated with death, doubt and mystery as in 'Else earth is darkness at the core,/And dust and ashes all that is,' (34). Although the drift of thought in that poem is positive, it is sapped by the despondent heaviness of the alliteration and the use of 'darkness at the core' in the couplet – the very 'core' of the poem. Other important words that also create uncertainty are 'seem' (three times), 'seemed' (four times), 'dim' (four times), and 'deep' (eight times). There are repeated words which are more expressive of hope: 'high' (6 times), 'higher' (10 times), 'felt' (9 times) and 'light' (29 times). The universal feel of the poem is partly the result of the use of 'vast' (3 times) and 'vaster' (5 times).

The last unifying feature is very important though not always easy to detect – the movement of the language. There is a characteristic verse music in the poem, which is marked by a sad, tired and sometimes despairing falling cadence. Sometimes the steady, even heavy, rhythm and the downward pitch in the intonation of a line express, particularly at a close, the weight of grief and perplexity:

And unto me no second friend. (6)

'Is this the end? Is this the end?' (12)

So many worlds, so much to do (73)

The leaden finality of the first, the weary repetition of the second in which, unusually, the voice naturally falls rather than rises with the question, and the burdened quality of the third are typical of the bleak music of *In Memoriam*. There are more affirmative cadences (the end of 95 is an obvious example), but even as late as poem 100 there is this lamenting close: 'I think once more he seems to die.'

4.3 THE INFLUENCE OF OTHER LITERATURE

A glance through the notes of an edition of *In Memoriam* reveals that
Tennyson constantly alludes to other literary works; there are
frequent references to the *Bible*, Latin poets such as Catullus
and Virgil, Dante's *La Divina Commedia*, and the English writers
alluded to read like a roll-call of the famous: Lord Byron, Thomas
Campbell, S. T. Coleridge, Abraham Cowley, William Cowper,
George Crabbe, Thomas Gray, George Herbert, John Keats, Christopher Marlowe, Andrew Marvell, John Milton, Alexander Pope,
Percy Bysshe Shelley and William Wordsworth. Above all there is
Shakespeare, whose plays and *Sonnets*, poems on the passing of time
and love which are mostly addressed to a male friend, are frequently
recalled.

Two points should be made about Tennyson's allusions. The first is
that it shouldn't be surprising; for generations English poets have
drawn on other writers, particularly Latin ones, for conventions and
themes. It is, then, a little surprising to note that A. C. Bradley
thought this might be an impediment to the reader's pleasure. He
concludes his section on 'Parallel Pasages' by saying that our pleasure
in Tennyson's phrasing 'is quite unaffected by the fact that he was
sometimes unconsciously indebted to his predecessors.' It may be that
some of the similarities are unconscious, but, in any case, there is no
need for such an excuse. In fact the second point can be made by
asserting that Tennyson often deliberately invites the reader to bear
in mind the heritage of thought and feeling enshrined in literature, so
that allusions to other works can establish the significance of his own.
Three examples will help to establish this.

Children of Tennyson's generation read (and probably wrote)
more in Latin than English. Latin, therefore, moulded their thoughts
and feelings. Hence, in one of the saddest poems – 57 – Tennyson
closes with an allusion to the elegy the Roman poet Catullus wrote
for his dead brother: 'Atque in perpetuum, frater, ave atque vale'
(And forever, O my brother, hail and farewell). Tennyson wrote:
'And "Ave, Ave, Ave," said,/"Adieu, adieu for evermore.' The
allusion creates strong crosscurrents of feeling. Catullus bade farewell
for ever, whereas Tennyson hails his friend three times before bidding
him 'adieu (a word less final than goodbye?). The presence of a word
actually used by Catullus points to the eternal separation of which the
Latin poet wrote, but Tennyson's repetition of 'Ave' might suggest a
closer relationship with the dead and even the possibility of a future
meeting.

The second and third examples are both from 7. The poet says this of himself: 'And like a guilty thing I creep/At earliest morning to the door.' The phrase 'like a guilty thing' comes directly from Shakespeare's *Hamlet*, where it refers to the ghost of Hamlet's father, which 'started like a guilty thing' at the return of dawn. The transference of a phrase about the dead to the living is eerily impressive; not only does death make the poet feel guilty (bereaved people often feel it is somehow wrong that they have survived) it reduces him to a ghost-like state. But if the loving poet feels like a ghost, what of the dead friend? The next stanza begins: 'He is not here; but far away/The noise of life begins again'. That is a bold move: 'He is not here' deliberately echoes words from *St Luke's Gospel* about the resurrected Christ – 'He is not here; but is risen (*St Luke* 24:6). There is, then, the promise of new life for the friend, yet against that there must be set the heavy break in the line before 'but' which is followed not by the triumphant 'is risen' but the remoteness of 'far away.' The poet is therefore left, as the bereaved often are, with a problem of location: is the friend risen and so with God or just so 'far away' as to be simply lost?

5 A CRITICAL READING OF POEM 95

5.1 POEM 95

By night we linger'd on the lawn,
    For underfoot the herb was dry;
    And genial warmth; and o'er the sky
The silvery haze of summer drawn;

And calm that let the tapers burn
    Unwavering: not a cricket chirr'd:
    The brook alone far-off was heard,
And on the board the fluttering urn:

And bats went round in fragrant skies,
    And wheel'd or lit the filmy shapes
    That haunt the dusk, with ermine capes
And woolly breasts and beaded eyes;

While now we sang old songs that peal'd
    From knoll to knoll, where, couch'd at ease,
    The white kine glimmer'd, and the trees
Laid their dark arms about the field.

But when those others, one by one,
    Withdrew themselves from me and night,
    And in the house light after light
Went out, and I was all alone,

A hunger seized my heart; I read
    Of that glad year which once had been,

In those fall'n leaves which kept their green,
The noble letters of the dead:

And strangely on the silence broke
    The silent-speaking words, and strange
    Was love's dumb cry defying change
To test his worth; and strangely spoke

The faith, the vigour, bold to dwell
    On doubts that drive the coward back,
    And keen through wordy snares to track
Suggestion to her inmost cell.

So word by word, and line by line,
    The dead man touch'd me from the past,
    And all at once it seem'd at last
The living soul was flash'd on mine,

And mine in this was wound, and whirl'd
    About empyreal heights of thought,
    And came on that which is, and caught
The deep pulsations of the world,

Æonian music measuring out
    The steps of Time – the shocks of Chance –
    The blows of Death. At length my trance
Was cancell'd, stricken through with doubt.

Vague words! but ah, how hard to frame
    In matter-moulded forms of speech,
    Or ev'n for intellect to reach
Through memory that which I became:

Till now the doubtful dusk reveal'd
    The knolls once more where, couch'd at ease,
    The white kine glimmer'd, and the trees
Laid their dark arms about the field:

And suck'd from out the distant gloom
    A breeze began to tremble o'er
    The large leaves of the sycamore,
And fluctuate all the still perfume,

And gathering freshlier overhead,
    Rock'd the full-foliaged elms, and swung
    The heavy-folded rose, and flung
The lilies to and fro, and said,

'The dawn, the dawn,' and died away;
    And East and West, without a breath,
    Mixt their dim lights, like life and death,
To broaden into boundless day.

5.2 CRITICISM

The subject of this poem is an experience of the mystical type in
which, for a moment, the poet establishes contact with his friend and
encounters the ultimate – 'that which is'. It is important because it
fulfils a longing for a meeting with the departed, and though it does
nor form a dramatic turning point, there is never again the numbing
despair of earlier poems.

The poem opens quietly with light alliterations, several long and
even languid vowels, and a sentence structure which, because it runs
over four stanzas and contains many clauses commencing with 'and',
creates a feeling of space and peace. As the scene widens and
expands, the people become passive, their main activity being that of
hearing – 'The brook alone far-off was heard'. Just how inactive they
become may be seen in the way the brook rather than people is the
subject of the passive verb. In fact, most of the verbs in the first four
stanzas don't have people for their subjects; for instance, 'the herb
was dry', 'and the trees/Laid their dark arms about the field.'

The effect of allaying human activity is twofold. First, although
people are not active, many of the senses are keenly aware, so the
mood created is receptive and contemplative. In feeling the 'genial
warmth', seeing 'The silvery haze', hearing the brook, smelling the
'fragrant skies' and acknowledging the presence of the 'woolly
breasts' of the bats, the senses are understood to be alert and, in the
case of the bats which are known to be woolly but not yet actually felt
to be so, anticipatory. This feeling of alertness and readiness for
experience is evident in the second effect. In an unobtrusive way the
landscape and atmosphere is gently symbolic of a spiritually receptive
soul: the candles ('tapers') that 'burn/Unwavering' suggest a soul in a
clear and untroubled state of responsiveness (the candle is a symbol
of the mind), and the distant sound of the brook may be intended to
touch off in the reader the suggestion of a soul intuiting the elusive

presence of God, water being a common symbol of spiritual refreshment. The whole scene is, indeed, suffused with religious suggestions: the bats wheel in circles (a symbol of perfection), and Tennyson employs Biblical language by calling the cattle 'kine'.

The word 'But' in line 17 heralds a change in mood. Up to this point the adjective 'dark' – 'laid their dark arms about the field' – has been the only suggestion of unease in a quiet, contemplative and even benign landscape. Now people leave, the house lights go out, and he is left, as the poet in Gray's 'Elegy' is, alone with the night. Is there in this scene the gentle pressure of a symbolic meaning? Is this the dark night of the soul (note the conjunction of 'me and night') in which spiritual comfort is withdrawn but which, if endured, can lead to illumination? (See the section on poems 67–72 on pp. 27–9).

The sixth stanza introduces a very strong word: 'A hunger *seized* my heart'. The poet is still a passive subject. The nature of this hunger is not entirely clear; it is obviously a strong desire to communicate with his friend, but it could also be a spiritual hunger, in which case his friend's letters, however 'green' they are, will not satisfy him. The possibility that the hunger is also spiritual is strengthened by the steady, almost stealthy, rhythms of the following two stanzas. The run-on lines and the sliding alliteration on the 's' draw the reader into a strange kind of communication with the mind of the departed. The words 'strangely . . . strange . . . strangely' help to characterise the paradoxes of 'silent-speaking words' and 'love's dumb cry', and these 'wordy snares' 'track/Suggestion to her inmost cell.' The process can easily bear a religious interpretation: paradox is central to religious language and the image of an inner cell is unmistakably spiritual.

The religious potential of the scene is realised in lines 33–44. The deliberate rhythms of 'word by word' and 'line by line' usher in the fulfilment of his longing: 'The dead man touch'd me from the past'. Throughout the poem 'touch' and 'touch'd' have acquired a deep pathos because they have expressed the contact the poet most desires. A touch, so certain, so physical and yet so fleeting, has come to be the highest form of love's confirmation – and now it is his. It is necessary to probe the latent religious implications to appreciate just how astonishing that line is. The risen Christ tells Mary Magdalene not to touch him, but the friend breaks through the intervening years to touch the poet.

The moment of personal reunion gives way to an explicitly religious encounter. The language, given the elusive subject matter, inevitably becomes vaguer. The instantaneous – 'all at once' – gives way to personal impression – 'it seem'd' – and then to the ultimate –

'The living soul was flash'd on mine.' Two things need to be said about that line. The first is that Tennyson altered it from 'His living soul'. Given that 'His' commenced the line and was therefore capitalised, it is not clear whether it applies to God or the friend. Tennyson might have preferred the definite article because, since it could mean a personal God or a world soul, it was religiously comprehensive. The second point is that, though the reference is vague, the line is more emotionally particularised because of 'flash'd'. Previously 'flash' or 'flash'd' have expressed the poet's desire to pass intuitively from the world of the living to the dead. In 41 he writes 'And flash at once, my friend, to thee.' This desire is fulfilled, but in a profounder way: the poet does not flash to his friend, 'The living soul' is flash'd on his.

The poet is also an object of actions performed by an unnamed other in the next stanza. The language is unspecific, yet a picture emerges. Divinity, if that term is not too specific, is evoked in images of height and depth and between them is 'that which is' – a core or centre of reality which can only be named in the most philosophically primitive vocabulary as blunt, uncharacterised existence. Since 'that which is' stands between height and depth it seems, like the centre of a circle, to be real but not spatial, and because it simply 'is' it seems detached from time. Yet, from this spaceless and timeless presence, the poet hears 'Aenonian music measuring out/The steps of Time – the shocks of Chance – The blows of Death.' The absence of 'and' means that this is not a dreary list of Time's hideous triumphs. The rhythm is measured, controlled, impressive and even majestic – and from the core of things the passage of time (a basic subject of *In Memoriam*) seems neither frightening nor meaningless, but a sweeping, fundamentally right, progress.

The vision doesn't last. His 'trance' (the word suggests it might be false) is 'stricken thro' with doubt.' Tennyson doesn't need to elaborate – 'doubt' was a very potent word in the 1840s. The poet's immediate reaction is concern for language – 'Vague words!' But he is not quite bereft. He again becomes conscious of the landscape (lines 49–52, echoing 13–16), and in a complex sentence which runs through the last five stanzas, a calm hope emerges. Out of the ambiguous 'distant gloom' (it looks dark but, in fact, dawn is here) there is 'suck'd' a 'breeze', which, of course, is a symbol of poetic inspiration. It gathers power, trembling 'o'er/The large leaves of the sycamore', fluctuating 'perfume' into the air, rocking 'the full-foliaged elms', swinging 'The heavy-folded rose' (an emblem of the poet turned in upon himself?) and flinging 'The lilies to and fro' until it proclaims 'The dawn, the dawn' before dying away. It should be read as a triumphant return to the poet of his lyrical gifts, gifts which he had lost when he had been struck by doubt.

The poet has thus endured three kinds of dark nights: the loss of his friend, the darkness of his spirit and the loss of poetic power. 95 is about the emergence from darkness into light of all three. The 'dead man' has 'touch'd him, he has come upon 'that which is' and his lyricism has been released. In the final lines 'East and West', 'life and death', symbols of spiritual reintegration and a permanent reunion, are mingled into a 'day', which, because it is 'boundless', is beyond death.

6 CRITICAL APPROACHES

The poem's intense popularity is critically important. Thousands of copies were sold, it was warmly reviewed, Queen Victoria, after the death of her husband Albert, gained much comfort from it, lines from it ('God's finger touch'd him and he slept') were used on tombstones, it was set to music, poems from it appeared in hymn-books, it was frequently quoted in sermons (the present author heard the last stanza of Epilogue quoted in a sermon in 1985) and phrases such as 'red in tooth and claw' entered the common language. A delightful example of the last point appears in an article on batting by the late Victorian and Edwardian cricketer Gilbert Jessop, a big hitter and fastest scoring batsman of all time, in which he says: 'It's better to have hit and missed than never to have hit at all.'

The academic seal of approval upon such popularity was given in 1901 with the publication of *A Commentary on Tennyson's 'In Memoriam'* by A. C. Bradley. Three things are important about it. The first is that it may be significant that Bradley published it *before* his *Shakespearean Tragedy*. Was this a case of first things first? The second is the title. Bradley's readers would be most familiar with the word 'commentary' from books about *The Bible*. The very word points to the religious significance that *In Memoriam* was felt to possess. The third significant thing is that in addition to chapters on the composition and structure of the poem, Bradley has one entitled 'The ideas used in *In Memoriam*.' That chapter opens with this question: 'How does Tennyson habitually think of the soul and its future, and on what does his faith appear to be based?' Bradley, in other words, took very seriously the intellectual thrust of the poem. In doing this he was, no doubt, being faithful to all those readers who found the poem not just a delight to the ear and the imagination but a serious meditation upon the ultimate questions of life.

In the early decades of the twentieth century Tennyson's reputation suffered. The fashion of attacking him produced one famous (notorious?) remark from a poet who, in some respects, rather resembled Tennyson – T. S. Eliot. In a deliberate effort to qualify the religious popularity of *In Memoriam* he wrote, in 1936, that 'It is not religious because of the quality of its faith, but because of the quality of its doubt. Its faith is a poor thing, but its doubt is a very intense experience.' It is important to see just how different a kind of judgement that is from Bradley's. To Bradley *In Memoriam* can be read as philosophy or teaching; to Eliot the poem is interesting not, to put it crudely, for what it says, but for the quality of mind evident in it.

The last 30 years have seen a revival of interest in Tennyson. W. W. Robson's essays showed just how interesting and problematic he was, and Christopher Ricks, in addition to a superb annotated edition of the complete works, showed that the verse was capable of being read in the close, analytic style popularised by practical criticism. Three approaches to the poem have emerged in this period: the scholarly, the linguistic and the cultural.

The scholarly approach has shown in detail how the poem took shape and how it is rich in allusions to other works. In 1976 Paul Turner's *Tennyson* was published. Its chapter on *In Memoriam* shows how the poem draws on Hallam's writings, Horace, Catullus, Petrarch, Shakespeare, Lucretius, Goethe, Dante, and writers on science. In 1982 the Susan Shatto and Marion Shaw edition of the poem was published. The detail of the commentary may be judged from the fact that it occupies nearly 150 pages. It is essential for any scholarly study of the poem.

The linguistic approach includes a scrupulous examination of the grammar, diction and imagery of the poem. The most detailed study is Alan Sinfield's *The Language of Tennyson's 'In Memoriam'*. He stresses the coexistence in the poem of an essentially romantic – personal, subjective – outlook with a more classical, stylised manner of writing. He also stresses how rich the diction of the poem is: 'My argument, then, is that beneath the apparently simple and unremarkable diction of *In Memoriam* are effects of great complexity resulting from the juxtaposition of quite ordinary words.'

The cultural approach sees what Tennyson is doing in the poem as symptomatic of the kind of attitudes to language that evolved in the nineteenth century. The stress is not so much on the meanings Tennyson makes but on the significance of his poetic strategies, particularly in relation to the larger question of how words generate meanings. Isobel Armstrong's *Language as Living Form in Nine-teenth Century Poetry* is an interesting example of this approach. She calls the language of nineteenth - century verse 'idealist' because 'it aims to make rather than copy'. Her closely argued case about *In Memoriam* is that it is a highly reflexive poem, constantly commenting upon itself in the way it searches for and then finds inadequate an appropriate poetic language.

What these three approaches do not tackle is the matter of the poem's thought. The Victorian reading public took it seriously, and so did Bradley. Perhaps, we shall not fully engage with *In Memoriam* until we ask basic questions about it: what does it say about the living and the dead, and is what is said true? The trouble is that the climate of modern criticism makes it easy to dodge such questions.

REVISION QUESTIONS

1. In what ways can *In Memoriam* be said to be a love poem?

2. 'The real subject of *In Memoriam* is the threat and the promise of time.' Do you agree?

3. *In Memoriam* has been called the way of the poet as well as the way of the soul. In what ways does the poem take an interest in poetry?

4. Write about how *In Memoriam* struggles to reconcile the view of 'Nature red in tooth and claw' with more positive understandings of the natural world.

5. What is the function in the poem of the cycle of the seasons, landscape and weather?

6. Do you agree that the poem's doubt is more impressive than the faith it expresses?

7. How successful are Tennyson's attempts in *In Memoriam* to deal with the discoveries of science?

8. Is *In Memoriam* an optimistic poem?

9. Is Tennyson more impressive when dealing with private or public matters?

10. Discuss the range and appropriateness of *In Memoriam's* stanza form.

11. Does *In Memoriam* have an over-all design and if so, what is it?

12. In what senses, if at all, can *In Memoriam* be said to be a unified poem?

13. 'A poem always in search of appropriate imagery.' Discuss the various images Tennyson employs to express the relationship between the poet and his dead friend.

14. Is it helpful to call *In Memoriam* a philosophical poem?

15. What kinds of changes does the poet in the poem undergo?

16. Do you find *In Memoriam* embarrassing because of its sentimentality?

17. 'The thought of *In Memoriam* is commonplace but its feelings are impressively expressed.' Discuss.

18. Does *In Memoriam* have an abiding apeal or is it merely a poetic document of a bygone age?

19. Should we praise *In Memoriam* for its variety of mood and subject matter or judge it unsuccessful because it monotonously concentrates on death and bereavement?

20. Why do you think *In Memoriam* was such a popular poem?

21. Can you suggest why many readers have found *In Memoriam* a consoling poem?

22. Are you in any way persuaded by the convictions reached by the poet in *In Memoriam*?

FURTHER READING

Editions

Ricks, Christopher (ed.), *The Poems of Tennyson* (Longman, 1969).
Shatto, Susan and Shaw, Marion (eds), *Tennyson 'In Memoriam*' (Clarendon Press, 1982).

Biography

Martin, Robert Bernard, *Tennyson: The Unquiet Heart* (Oxford University Press and Faber & Faber, 1983).
Tennyson, Charles, *Alfred Tennyson* (Macmillan, 1949).

Criticism

Armstrong, Isobel, *Language as Living Form in Nineteenth Century Poetry* (Harvester, 1982).
Bradley, A. C., *A Commentary on Tennyson's 'In Memoriam'* (Macmillan, 1901).
Culler A., Dwight *The Poetry of Tennyson* (Yale, 1977).
Gransden, K. W., *Tennyson 'In Memoriam'* (Arnold, 1964).
Hunt, John Dixon (ed.), *Tennyson 'In Memoriam' (a Casebook)* (Macmillan, 1970).
Robson, W.W., *Critical Essays* (Routledge & Kegan Paul, 1966).
Shaw, W. David, *Tennyson's Style* (Cornell University Press, 1976).
Sinfield, Alan, *The Language of Tennyson's 'In Memoriam'* (Blackwell, 1971).
Turner, Paul, *Tennyson* (Routledge & Kegan Paul, 1976).
Willey, Basil, *More Nineteenth Century Studies* (Chatto & Windus, 1963).

Mastering English Literature
Richard Gill

Mastering English Literature will help readers both to enjoy English Literature and to be successful in 'O' levels, 'A' levels and other public exams. It is an introduction to the study of poetry, novels and drama which helps the reader in four ways – by providing ways of approaching literature, by giving examples and practice exercises, by offering hints on how to write about literature, and by the author's own evident enthusiasm for the subject. With extracts from more than 200 texts, this is an enjoyable account of how to get the maximum satisfaction out of reading, whether it be for formal examinations or simply for pleasure.

Work Out English Literature ('A' level)
S.H. Burton

This book familiarises 'A' level English Literature candidates with every kind of test which they are likely to encounter. Suggested answers are worked out step by step and accompanied by full author's commentary. The book helps students to clarify their aims and establish techniques and standards so that they can make appropriate responses to similar questions when the examination pressures are on. It opens up fresh ways of looking at the full range of set texts, authors and critical judgements and motivates students to know more of these matters.

THE MACMILLAN SHAKESPEARE

General Editor: PETER HOLLINDALE
Advisory Editor: PHILIP BROCKBANK

The Macmillan Shakespeare features:
* clear and uncluttered texts with modernised punctuation and spelling wherever possible;
* full explanatory notes printed on the page facing the relevant text for ease of reference;
* stimulating introductions which concentrate on content, dramatic effect, character and imagery, rather than mere dates and sources.

Above all, The Macmillan Shakespeare treats each play as a work for the theatre which can also be enjoyed on the page.

CORIOLANUS
Editor: Tony Parr

THE WINTER'S TALE
Editor: Christopher Parry

MUCH ADO ABOUT NOTHING
Editor: Jan McKeith

RICHARD II
Editor: Richard Adams

RICHARD III
Editor: Richard Adams

HENRY IV, PART I
Editor: Peter Hollindale

HENRY IV, PART II
Editor: Tony Parr

HENRY V
Editor: Brian Phythian

AS YOU LIKE IT
Editor: Peter Hollindale

A MIDSUMMER NIGHT'S DREAM
Editor: Norman Sanders

THE MERCHANT OF VENICE
Editor: Christopher Parry

THE TAMING OF THE SHREW
Editor: Robin Hood

TWELFTH NIGHT
Editor: E. A. J. Honigmann

THE TEMPEST
Editor: A. C. Spearing

ROMEO AND JULIET
Editor: James Gibson

JULIUS CAESAR
Editor: D. R. Elloway

MACBETH
Editor: D. R. Elloway

HAMLET
Editor: Nigel Alexander

ANTONY AND CLEOPATRA
Editors: Jan McKeith and
Richard Adams

OTHELLO
Editors: Celia Hilton and R. T. Jones

KING LEAR
Editor: Philip Edwards

MACMILLAN STUDENTS' NOVELS

General Editor: JAMES GIBSON

The Macmillan Students' Novels are low-priced, new editions of major classics, aimed at the first examination candidate. Each volume contains:

* enough explanation and background material to make the novels accessible — and rewarding — to pupils with little or no previous knowledge of the author or the literary period;

* detailed notes elucidate matters of vocabulary, interpretation and historical background;

* eight pages of plates comprising facsimiles of manuscripts and early editions, portraits of the author and photographs of the geographical setting of the novels.

JANE AUSTEN: MANSFIELD PARK
Editor: Richard Wirdnam

JANE AUSTEN: NORTHANGER ABBEY
Editor: Raymond Wilson

JANE AUSTEN: PRIDE AND PREJUDICE
Editor: Raymond Wilson

JANE AUSTEN: SENSE AND SENSIBILITY
Editor: Raymond Wilson

JANE AUSTEN: PERSUASION
Editor: Richard Wirdnam

CHARLOTTE BRONTË: JANE EYRE
Editor: F. B. Pinion

EMILY BRONTË: WUTHERING HEIGHTS
Editor: Graham Handley

JOSEPH CONRAD: LORD JIM
Editor: Peter Hollindale

CHARLES DICKENS: GREAT EXPECTATIONS
Editor: James Gibson

CHARLES DICKENS: HARD TIMES
Editor: James Gibson

CHARLES DICKENS: OLIVER TWIST
Editor: Guy Williams

CHARLES DICKENS: A TALE OF TWO CITIES
Editor: James Gibson

GEORGE ELIOT: SILAS MARNER
Editor: Norman Howlings

GEORGE ELIOT: THE MILL ON THE FLOSS
Editor: Graham Handley

D. H. LAWRENCE: SONS AND LOVERS
Editor: James Gibson

D. H. LAWRENCE: THE RAINBOW
Editor: James Gibson

MARK TWAIN: HUCKLEBERRY FINN
Editor: Christopher Parry